WALTHER MODEL

LEADERSHIP ■ STRATEGY ■ CONFLICT

ROBERT FORCYZK ■ ILLUSTRATED BY ADAM HOOK

First published in 2011 by Osprey Publishing
Midland House, West Way, Botley, Oxford OX2 0PH, UK
44-02 23rd St, Suite 219, Long Island City, NY 11101, USA

E-mail: info@ospreypublishing.com

ISBN: 978 1 84908 357 7
E-book ISBN: 978 1 84908 358 4

Editorial by Ilios Publishing Ltd, Oxford, UK
Cartography: Mapping Specialists Ltd
Page Layouts by Myriam Bell Design, France
Typeset in Stone Serif and Officina Sans
Index by Alan Thatcher
Originated by United Graphic Pte Ltd
Printed in China through Worldprint Ltd.

11 12 13 14 15   10 9 8 7 6 5 4 3 2 1

www.ospreypublishing.com

Acknowledgments

I wish to thank Nik Cornish, Ian Barter and the Bundesarchiv for their
help with this project.

Dedication

In remembrance of Lt. Salvatore S. Corma, A/2-508 IN, 82nd Airborne
Division, died of wounds in Zabul Province, Afghanistan, 29 April 2010.

Artist's note

Readers may care to note that the original paintings from which the
colour plates in this book were prepared are available for private sale.
All reproduction copyright whatsoever is retained by the Publishers.
All enquiries should be addressed to:

Scorpio Gallery, PO Box 475, Hailsham, East Sussex BN27 2SL, UK

The Publishers regret that they can enter into no correspondence upon
this matter.

Front cover image

Author's collection.

Back cover images

Ian Barter.

The Woodland Trust

Osprey Publishing are supporting the Woodland Trust, the UK's leading
woodland conservation charity, by funding the dedication of trees.

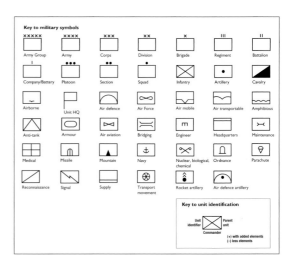

CONTENTS

INTRODUCTION

I love him, who strives for the impossible.
Johann Wolfgang von Goethe (Faust II, 1832)

Surrounded by adversaries, German armies have traditionally cultivated the concept of *Bewegungskrieg* (manoeuvre warfare) as the optimal solution to military problems. Clausewitz had argued that only offensive operations could provide decisive results and that the logical conclusion of *Stellungskrieg* (positional warfare) was defeat, so German military tradition favoured offensive tactics. However, the failure of the offensive Schlieffen Plan to achieve a quick knockout in France in August 1914 forced the Imperial German Army onto the defensive for the next four years. Despite a doctrinal focus on *Bewegungskrieg*, the German Army on the Western Front proved masterful on the defence, coordinating artillery, machine guns, barbed-wire obstacles and multiple switch lines to impede, bloody and then stop powerful Allied offensives in Flanders, the Somme and Champagne. During the autumn of 1916 the German Army codified the lessons learned from these successful defensive operations into the doctrine of 'elastic defence'. Unlike previous defensive doctrines, which emphasized placing all available manpower in a rigid linear defence, elastic defence spread out manpower across three successive zones, which made them less vulnerable to massive artillery barrages. Although German military thinking remained wedded to offensive solutions and tactics, elastic defence proved to be an effective doctrine in 1917–18. During this period, a young German officer named Walther Model experienced at first hand the effectiveness of elastic defence at both the tactical and operational levels – experience he would later put to good use when he became one of the Wehrmacht's most important operational commanders in the next war.

In the post-war Reichswehr, elastic defence was retained in the 1921 operations manual and updated to incorporate anti-tank defences in 1933. However, both the Reichswehr and the Wehrmacht returned to an offensive mindset, and elastic defence was relegated to the background, since Germany's new leader, Adolf Hitler, did not expect to fight defensive campaigns. This offensive spirit of the Wehrmacht carried the day in the opening years of World War II and cemented the reputations of commanders such as Manstein, Guderian, Rommel and Kleist. However, when the blitzkrieg culminated in the vastness of the Soviet Union and its spearheads failed to take Moscow, Leningrad or Stalingrad, the Wehrmacht suddenly found itself on the strategic defensive against an implacable foe – the Red Army – which began to relentlessly push German armies back towards the Fatherland. At this crisis point in the war, when German military power began to show signs of cracking, Walther Model arose to take command of the most critical fronts and time and again bought vital time for the Third Reich to recover. Model built his reputation as a successful defensive fighter against long odds and he rose from a division commander to an army commander in less than two years. Then, in March 1944, Hitler made him the youngest *Generalfeldmarschall* in the Wehrmacht. Like most German commanders in Russia, Model found that the elastic defence doctrine was not really applicable on such a vast front, but he succeeded in developing a type of zone defence that matched his available resources. Although some staff officers resented his brusque style, the common German *Landser* (soldier) took comfort that whenever Walther Model arrived to take command of their sector he would bring some semblance of order and stability out of chaos and retreat.

Unlike most other German senior commanders, Model also enjoyed a good relationship with the Führer and never joined the anti-Hitler conspiracy. In return, Hitler openly considered Model his best field commander and praised him as his 'fireman', who could be shifted from one collapsing front to another in order to retrieve seemingly hopeless situations. While Model's efforts could not reverse the Third Reich's overall deteriorating military situation, he did demonstrate a flair for battlefield improvisation that continually confounded Germany's enemies. Model was unique in inflicting serious defeats upon Marshal Georgy Zhukov in the Rzhev salient in November 1942, Field Marshal Bernard Montgomery at Arnhem in September 1944 and Lieutenant-General Omar Bradley in the Hürtgen Forest and the Ardennes in November–December 1944. Although Model is not as well known as the commanders who won their spurs during the heady days of blitzkrieg in 1939–41, it was he and a few other defensive experts, including Erhard Raus and Hans-Valentin Hube, who were able to slow, if not stop, the inexorable tide of the Allied and Soviet armies advancing towards Berlin.

Model (in the centre of the back row) as a *Fähnrich* in 1910. As a small, non-athletic youth with poor eyesight, Model did not appear to conform to the ideal stereotype of a Prussian officer, but his regimental commander took a chance and accepted him for training. This proved to be the beginning of a brilliant 35-year military career. (Author)

THE EARLY YEARS, 1891–1913

In January 1891, Otto Moritz Walther Model was born in the quiet farming town of Genthin, located 80km west of Berlin. His father, Otto Paul Moritz Model, who taught music in the local girls' school, and his mother, Marie Pauline Wilhelmine, née Demmer, came from a bourgeois background. An elder brother, Otto (1884–1964), was seven years older than Walther. When Walther was five years old his family moved into a single-room lodging. Unlike most German *Generalfeldmarschalle,* Model not only came from a non-military family with no ties to the landed gentry, but his early years were spent in austere conditions, with limited running water in the house.

Walther was raised in the German evangelical church and initially attended the village school in Genthin. In 1900 Model's father became a music director in Erfurt, and Walther attended the gymnasium there for the next six years. After years of moving around and living in temporary lodgings, the Model family finally settled in Naumburg. In school, Walther took no interest in sports but joined a literary society and showed an aptitude for Latin, Greek, history and poetry. However, Naumburg had a distinctly military atmosphere compared to Genthin or Erfurt, with a regiment of infantry and artillery garrisoned in the town. Several of Walther's schoolmates were the sons of army officers and invited him to witness the drills of the local infantry regiment. One of Walther's friends was Hans-Valentin Hube, the son of an army *Oberst*. In February 1909, Walther was one of 19 students in his *Gymnasium* who passed the examination committee and received their *Abitur*. Of these graduates, Walther, Hans Hube and five others opted to join the Army.

Walther's decision to join the Army came as something of a surprise to his non-military family, who had expected him to go on to law school like his older brother Otto. It was not easy for someone coming from a non-military background to gain access to the officer accession process in the Kaiser's Army, so Walther sought help from his uncle Martin Model, a reserve officer in Infanterie-Regiment von Alvensleben Nr. 52. Using his contacts, Martin was able to get young Walther an interview with his regimental commander, Oberst Henseling. Three days after he gained his *Abitur*, Walther went with his father by train to Cottbus. Standing before Oberst Henseling, Walther Model – short, unathletic and myopic – did not appear to fit the ideal of a Prussian officer, but Henseling was impressed by the young man's attitude and decided to accept him as an officer cadet (*Fahnenjunker*) in the regiment.

As was normal in the German Army, Walther spent the next eight months learning basic drill and NCO responsibilities in III Batallion, and then, having demonstrated sufficient aptitude, was promoted to the rank of *Fähnrich* (ensign) in November 1909 and sent to the *Kriegsschule* (military school) in Neisse. Model sailed through the course and returned to his regiment as a newly minted *Leutnant* in August 1910. He spent the next three years as a company-level officer, learning his trade as an infantryman.

During this period, Model repeatedly demonstrated high levels of enthusiasm, efficiency and zest in completing tasks, which his superiors noticed. When a battalion adjutant position became vacant in October 1913, Leutnant Model was chosen even though he was still a very junior officer. It was this role that allowed Model to showcase his talents and gain recognition from his superiors. As battalion adjutant, Model began to adopt the mannerisms of a traditional Prussian officer – a stern demeanour accented by a prominent monocle – but retained the work ethic and speech of a German small-town bourgeois.

THE MILITARY LIFE, 1914–41

World War I, 1914–18

When World War I began in August 1914, Leutnant Model's regiment played a major role in the invasion of Belgium. On 23 August 1914 Model had his baptism of fire when his regiment conducted a frontal attack against the British Expeditionary Force at Mons and was repulsed with heavy losses. However, after the march on Paris failed because of the Allied counter-attack on the Marne in early September, Model's regiment reverted to trench warfare around Soissons.

Although Model spent his first year in combat without attracting much attention, his first opportunity for recognition came in the autumn of 1915. The French were determined to push the German forces out of their country and began massing over 2,000 artillery pieces for a grand offensive in Champagne. Model's regiment was squarely in the path of this onslaught. On 21 September 1915 Oberleutnant Model was in his battalion command post on the reverse slope of the Butte de Tahure, located 41km east of Reims, when the French began a massive 75-hour artillery preparation. After three days of pounding, the IIe Corps d'Armée Colonial – one of the toughest units in the French Army – attacked the German trenches on the Butte but was thrown back with heavy losses. In the aftermath of the attack,

German troops in waterlogged trenches, autumn 1915. Model's introduction to trench warfare began in Champagne, where he was wounded twice in 1915. Virtually all of Model's experience in World War I was based on positional defensive combat. (Ian Barter)

Model coolly sent a report to the brigade commander, Oberst Prince Oskar von Preussen, which said: 'Infantry ammunition expended. Frenchmen are pushed back. At present, 60 per cent of our regiment is disabled. Please send immediate support.' The prince, who was one of the Kaiser's sons, was impressed by Model's coolness under pressure and duly dispatched reinforcements. He also made a note to recommend Model for Großer Generalstab (General Staff) training. For his combat performance on the Butte de Tahure, Oberleutnant Model was awarded the Iron Cross 1st Class on 19 October. However, after the French offensive ended Model was seriously wounded by artillery fragments in his right shoulder on 3 November 1915. He spent six weeks in hospital recuperating.

Model returned to his adjutant duties before Christmas in 1915, and his unit was selected to participate in the upcoming Verdun offensive. On 25 April 1916 Model was badly wounded in the right thigh by shell fragments. When he returned to the front, Prince Oskar made him his brigade adjutant. Model continued to demonstrate great skill as a staff officer and in June 1917 Oberst Hans von Seeckt selected him to join the Oberste Heeresleitung (OHL), the Army supreme command. Leutnant Model served as an ordnance officer in the OHL at Bad Kreuznach until February 1918, when Seeckt and Prince Oskar recommended Model for Großer Generalstab training. He then went to Sedan for a month-long abbreviated course. This was an important point in Model's career and meant that he had been identified as someone with (higher) command potential. After completing the course, Model was sent to become the Ib (supply) officer for the Garde-Ersatz-Division for the 1918 Spring Offensive. However, after the German offensives culminated and failed to win the war, he was assigned as Ib officer of the 36. Reserve-Division, stationed in Flanders for the remaining months of the war. Model gained considerable combat and staff experience during World War I, as well as surviving three combat wounds.

A German soldier throwing grenades at Verdun, in 1916. Model learned his infantry tactics in the school of hard knocks at Verdun, where he developed a hardened attitude towards casualties, which others later interpreted as callousness. (Ian Barter)

Service in the Reichswehr, 1919–35

Despite admission to the prestigious Großer Generalstab, Model was bitter about Germany's defeat, and the prospects for a post-war military career appeared grim. Model spent the next year uncertain if he would remain in the Army, but in November 1919 he found out that he was one of the 4,000 Army officers Generaloberst Hans von Seeckt

Left: Oberleutnant Model (left) with the OHL at Bad Kreuznach, in the autumn of 1917. Generalfeldmarschall Paul von Hindenburg and General Erich Ludendorff are in the centre. Being assigned to the OHL was a tremendous career break for young Model, and he became a protégé of Oberst Hans von Seeckt. (Author)

had selected to remain in the down-sized Reichswehr, as mandated by the Treaty of Versailles.

Model was appointed as a company commander in the 14. (Badisches) Infanterie-Regiment stationed in Konstanz on the Swiss border. In March 1920 his unit was sent to the Ruhr to suppress an armed communist uprising in the town of Eberfeld; over 1,000 strikers were shot by the Reichswehr. While quartered in civilian housing in the Ruhr he met Herta Huyssen (1892–1985). One year later they were married in Frankfurt on 11 May 1921. By this point Model had been transferred to Wehrkreis VI, where he commanded another infantry company for a year in Gorlitz and then served as a Großer Generalstab officer in Münster for four years. During this period, Model's daughter Hella was born in September 1923.

While in Münster, Model worked for General der Infanterie 'Fritz' von Loßberg, the commander of Wehrkreis VI and a skilled defensive tactician from World War I. Loßberg became one of Model's most important professional mentors, and the young *Hauptmann* was impressed by Loßberg's concept of 'defence in depth'. During World War I, Loßberg had displayed a particular talent for helping to restore German front lines that were nearly broken by Allied offensives through the proper use of reserves and counter-attacks. Unlike other German officers, Loßberg opposed the doctrine of elastic defence and argued for a rigid, continuous front as essential to a successful defence against a strong enemy offensive.

Below: Heavily armed German communist 'Red Army' troops mobilize during the *Ruhraufstand* (Ruhr Uprising) in March 1920. Model's Reichswehr battalion was one of the units that was called in to crush the communist uprising and was involved in heavy, no-quarter fighting in Eberfeld. (Bundesarchiv, Bild 183-R99870)

After learning a great deal from Loßberg, Model was transferred to Wehrkreis III (Berlin) in 1925 to command another infantry company for three years, and was then assigned to the staff of 3. Division for one year. His son Hans-George was born in 1927 and another daughter, Christa, in 1929.

In October 1929 Model was promoted to the rank of *Major* and assigned to the Truppenamt (Troop Office) T4 (training) section in Berlin, where he put his Großer Generalstab training to good use. Model spent the next four years there, directing junior-level leadership training. His boss was Oberst Walther von Brauchitsch, who would later rise to become commander-in-chief of the Army; Model's association with Brauchitsch was another lucky break in his career. In August 1931 Model accompanied Brauchitsch on a six-week inspection trip to the covert training sites established in the Soviet Union, which were designed to evade the restrictions of the Treaty of Versailles. Model's reputation for hard work paid off, and in November 1932 he was promoted to the rank of *Oberstleutnant*.

Above: Hauptmann Model as a company commander stationed in Stuttgart in the post-war Reichswehr, summer 1920. Model was disillusioned by Germany's defeat in World War I and briefly considered leaving the military. However, his career was carefully guided by a series of professional mentors, including Seeckt, 'Fritz' Loßberg and Brauchitsch, to form the energetic young man into a polished Großer Generalstab officer. (Author)

Opposite: Reichswehr troops taking the Führereid (oath of loyalty to Adolf Hitler) in August 1934. For Model and most other German officers, the Führereid bound them to the Nazi regime, as Hitler intended. (Bundesarchiv, Bild 102-16108A)

After four years of staff duty in Berlin, it was time for Model to return to a troop assignment, and he was sent to command an infantry battalion in East Prussia during 1933–34. This was a period of great change for Germany, as Adolf Hitler became chancellor in 1933 and then commander-in-chief of the military in 1934. As Hitler pushed for lifting the restrictions of the Treaty of Versailles, conscription was reintroduced in March 1935 and the Reichswehr was superseded by the new Wehrmacht. In October 1934 Model was promoted to the rank of *Oberst* and took command of a regiment for a one-year tour.

Wehrmacht service, 1935–39

Another change brought by Hitler was the resurrection of the Großer Generalstab and the creation of the Oberkommando des Heeres (OKH). In October 1935 Model became chief of the 8th Department (Technical) of the Generalstab des Heeres (Army General Staff). He was responsible for inspecting, testing and evaluating new weaponry, particularly artillery. Model spent the next three years in this assignment and was promoted to the rank of *Generalmajor* in February 1938. He also became a strong advocate for Army motorization and he began his association with the nascent Panzer community while working in the Generalstab by siding with Generalleutnant Heinz Guderian on equipment and organization issues.

Unlike most of his peers, Model was not upset by the Blomberg-Fritsch affair in January 1938, in which the Nazi party gradually began to weed out political enemies from the Großer Generalstab. Indeed, the ascension of Walther von Brauchitsch – Model's old mentor from the Truppenamt – to become the new commander-in-chief of the Wehrmacht was a definite plus for Model's career prospects. Rather than buck the rising Nazi tide, Model astutely accepted that he had to kneel before their broken cross and began developing high-level social contacts among the Nazi elite, including Hermann Göring and Josef Goebbels. Rather than a political ideologue, Model was an ardent German nationalist and viewed the Nazi's party's programmes of rebuilding the military and dispensing with the restrictions of the Treaty of Versailles as necessary for restoring Germany's national dignity. Coming from a middle-class background, Model was also more appealing to the new Nazi leadership, and his distance from the old Prussian *Junker* class proved to be an asset.

Poland and France, 1939–40

In November 1938 Generalmajor Model was assigned as *Chef des Generalstabes* (Chief of Staff) of IV Armeekorps in Dresden. When the invasion of Poland began on 1 September 1939 Model's corps formed part of the southern pincer converging on Warsaw and was involved in the battle for the Czestochowa *Kessel* (pocket). However, during the two weeks of active campaigning in Poland, Model was more involved with mopping-up operations than blitzkrieg-style actions.

After the Polish campaign, Model was reassigned as *Chef des Generalstabes* of 16. Armee (AOK 16), commanded by General der Infanterie Ernst Busch. Model spent most of the winter of 1939–40 preparing for the campaign against France, which was postponed until the spring. In April 1940 Model was promoted to the rank of *Generalleutnant*. Once the invasion of France began on 10 May 1940, Busch's AOK 16 advanced through the Ardennes Forest, and, after the critical breakthrough at Sedan, helped to guard the left flank of Panzergruppe Kleist and fix the French 2e Armée in the Maginot Line. In the 39-day campaign, Model's responsibilities were an order of magnitude larger than in Poland, but his operational-level experience of warfare was still positional in nature.

Once France was occupied, AOK 16 switched to preparations for Operation *Seelöwe*, the intended invasion of Great Britain, in which Busch's army was tasked with landings near Dover. Model was actively involved in training for *Seelöwe* until the operation was postponed in September. Model was desperate to get a field command and his connections with Brauchitsch finally paid off; on 1 October 1940 he learned that he would receive command of the 3. Panzer-Division.

Above: Hauptmann Model with his company, 9./Infanterie-Regiment 8, during summer manoeuvres in 1927. Throughout his career, even when rubbing shoulders with the highest levels of the Großer Generalstab, Model always retained the blunt speech and direct mannerisms of an infantry leader, which did not always endear him to some of the 'softer' rear-echelon officers. (Author)

Commander of the 3. Panzer-Division

On 18 October 1940 Model arrived in Buckow, in the southeast suburbs of Berlin, to take command of the 3. Panzer-Division. The division was refitting and reorganizing in Wehrkreis III during the winter of 1940. Soon afterwards, Model was informed that his division would participate in Operation *Barbarossa*, the impending invasion of the Soviet Union. Model dived straight into a tough training regime for the division.

The 3. Panzer-Division was one of 17 Panzer divisions initially assigned to participate in Operation *Barbarossa*, and Model was one of only five commanders with no previous experience in Panzer units – a factor that caused some resentment. Despite coming from a non-Panzer background, at the age of 50 Model was in his peer group; his old classmate, Hans-Valentin Hube, took command of the 16. Panzer-Division at the same time. For *Barbarossa*, Model's division was assigned to XXIV Armeekorps (mot.) in Generaloberst Heinz Guderian's Panzergruppe 2. The 3. Panzer-Division was a veteran outfit fully equipped with 215 tanks. Indeed, this was the only time in his wartime military career that Model would command a full-strength unit, manned by veterans. Furthermore, unlike his supporting role in the Polish and French campaigns, this time Model would be in a key command spot in the spearhead of Heeresgruppe Mitte (Army Group Centre).

When the invasion began on 22 June 1941, Model's first task was to seize a crossing over the river Bug, south of the Soviet fortress of Brest-Litovsk. Model formed a special assault group of infantry and pioneers to seize the Koden Bridge, and it was captured intact 20 minutes before the actual commencement of hostilities. After the bridgehead was secure, Model moved quickly across in an Sd. Kfz. 232 (8-Rad) heavy armoured car and joined his spearhead. Model's division soon ran into the Soviet 22nd Tank Division, which was caught still in garrison and overrun. Model's Panzers destroyed 190 T-26 light tanks in the first 24 hours. Expanding from the Koden bridgehead, the 3. Panzer-Division skirted along the northern edge of the Pripet marshes and advanced eastward towards the town of Slutsk, on the direct route to Smolensk. Model faced more resistance from the terrain – including swamps, roadless morasses and endless river crossings – in the initial stages of the invasion than he did from the Red Army.

Model led from the front, often in his 8-Rad, with a mixed *Kampfgruppe* of Panzers, motorcycle infantry and motorized pioneers. His staff trailed behind him, trying to keep control over a division that was soon spread out in a long column and constantly running short of fuel.

Model served as chief of staff for General der Infanterie Ernst Busch's AOK 16 during the 1940 campaign in France. Busch was a solid but unimaginative commander who was willing to let Model do the heavy lifting for him, which suited his ambitious subordinate. Later, Model would replace Busch as commander of Heeresgruppe Mitte after the Soviet Operation *Bagration* shattered it in June 1944. (Author)

After advancing over 250km, Model reached the river Shchara late on 24 June. His main opponent – General-Major Stepan I. Oborin, commander of the 14th Mechanized Corps – burned the bridge over the river and, as the German pioneers built a new bridge, Soviet artillery bombarded the stalled German column. Model was standing outside his 8-Rad, observing the engineer's work, when artillery fire destroyed his nearby command vehicle. Nonplussed, Model urged his engineers to complete the bridge during the night and the next morning his Panzers were across. Model followed close behind the assault troops in a Pz III Befehlspanzer; this vehicle was also knocked out by Soviet fire but Model emerged unscathed. Oborin's corps was scattered and he was recalled to Moscow in disgrace and then executed. On 26 June Model arrived with the spearhead in Slutsk, having advanced 310km in four days. Not pausing, Model pushed on to the river Berezina two days later. Soon after this, Model was awarded the Knight's Cross for his accomplishments in the first two weeks of Operation *Barbarossa*.

By this point, the Soviet Western Front was reeling from the catastrophic encirclement of most of its forces at Minsk and had few forces at hand to stop Guderian's onrushing Panzers. On the evening of 3 July Model's division reached the river Dnepr at Rogachev, although fuel shortages prevented any further advance. After the heady advance of late June, the 3. Panzer-Division spent most of July and August slugging its way towards Roslavl and then Gomel. On 18 August Model ran into better-equipped Soviet armour units for the first time, when a unit of T-34 tanks counter-attacked at Unecha, but his better-trained Panzer crews prevailed. Just as the battles around Smolensk were winding down, Hitler redirected Panzergruppe Guderian southward to assist Heeresgruppe Süd (Army Group South) encircle the Soviet forces in Kiev.

Model's division advanced southwards on the morning of 23 August, and caught the Red Army by surprise, enabling his lead *Kamfgruppe* to seize intact the bridge over the river Desna. However, the Soviet 21st Army barred

Model commanded the 3. Panzer-Division during the first four months of the invasion of the Soviet Union. This formation had over 4,300 vehicles, including 100 Pz III medium tanks. Despite being new to the Panzerwaffe, Model proved himself a daring leader of armoured forces. (Ian Barter)

Above: Generalleutnant Model at the start of Operation *Barbarossa*. Although new to the Panzerwaffe, Model took to his new command with relish and quickly mastered the techniques of mobile warfare. (Author)

further progress southward and Model had to spend three weeks shoving his way forward against increasing resistance. Nevertheless, Model's luck held and his troops captured bridges over the river Sejm and river Sula, enabling his spearhead to link up with Hube's 16. Panzer-Division south of Lokhvitza on 15 September, which completed the encirclement of 55 Soviet divisions in the Kiev pocket. Thus, after a 350km advance, Model's division played a key role in the greatest German battle of encirclement in Operation *Barbarossa*.

Drive on Moscow 1941

Model was given no time to rest his worn-out division, which had fewer than 50 tanks left operational. Hitler decided to resume the advance on Moscow with Operation *Typhoon*, and Guderian was ordered to turn his *Panzergruppe* around and form the southern pincer of Heeresgruppe Mitte's new offensive, set to begin in just two weeks. The Führer's directive required Guderian's Panzers to move over 200km northwards to the vicinity of Kursk. When the offensive began on 30 September, Panzergruppe Guderian easily overran Group Ermakov in front of them and Model's division demolished the Soviet 121st Tank Brigade in short order. Guderian's Panzers then made a spectacular dash to seize Orel on 3 October, but at the cost of exhausting their remaining fuel. Model's division was stranded outside Orel for nearly a week, with nothing standing between them and the southern approaches to Moscow. As the 3. Panzer-Division awaited fuel near Orel, Model learned that he had been promoted to the rank of *General der Panzertruppe* and assigned command of XXXXI Armeekorps (mot.) in Generaloberst George-Hans Reinhardt's Panzergruppe 3 for the second phase of Operation *Typhoon*. Model arrived to take command of the corps on 29 October, just before the offensive was resumed.

Right: Model's forward command post south of Mogilev, around 5 July 1941. Model led from the front, often in an armoured car or halftrack, which enabled him to outmanoeuvre his Soviet opponents during the early stages of Operation *Barbarossa*. (Author)

Model's campaigns in the east, 1941–44

Legend:

Events

⑥ (numbered event marker)

↓ (arrow)

Panther Stellung
3. Panzer-Division 1941
XXXXI Armeekorps (mot.) 1941–1942
9. AOK 1942–1943
Heeresgruppe Nord 1944
Heeresgruppe Nordukraine 1944
Heeresgruppe Mitte 1944

0 — 200km
0 — 200 miles

1. 22 June – 26 October 1941: Model commands the 3. Panzer-Division in the opening months of Operation *Barbarossa*.

2. 1 November 1941 – 15 January 1942: Model is given command of XXXXI Armeekorps (mot.) for the final advance upon Moscow, which falls short of its objective.

3. 16 January 1942 – 30 March 1943: Model commands the 9. Armee (9 AOK) and successfully defends the Rzhev salient for over a year against ferocious Soviet attacks.

4. 1 April – 1 November 1943: Model's 9 AOK switches to the Orel Salient and he commands the northern pincer during the *Zitadelle* offensive in July 1943, then conducts a fighting withdrawl from Orel back to the Hagen Stellung.

5. 31 January – 30 March 1944: Model is given command of Heeresgruppe Nord after the Soviet breakout from Leningrad and he conducts a delaying retreat to the Panther Stellung.

6. 31 March – 28 June 1944: Model switches to command Heeresgruppe Nordukraine after Hitler relieves Manstein for failing to stop the Soviet advance to the Ukraine.

7. 28 June – 15 August 1944: While retaining command of Heeresgruppe Nordukraine, Model is given command of Heeresgruppe Mitte and succeeds in rebuilding a new front line in Poland after the Soviet Operation *Bagration* inflicts a crushing defeat on the Wehrmacht.

During this second phase of Operation *Typhoon*, Model had the thankless job of protecting Reinhardt's extended flank and maintaining a connection with 9. Armee (AOK 9) while the rest of Panzergruppe 3 advanced eastwards towards Klin. Soviet counterattacks relentlessly pounded AOK 9 and Model's corps. When the German advance stopped 40km short of Moscow, Reinhardt put Model in charge of the final push and gave him the the 6. Panzer-Division as well. Model remained optimistic about a breakthrough, but the final German attacks could not break the line held by Konstantin Rokossovsky's 16th Army. Once *Typhoon* culminated because of supply shortages, exhaustion and increased Soviet resistance, Reinhardt's Panzergruppe 3 found itself exposed in a salient with only screening forces protecting its northern flank.

Model with some of his key staff from the 3. Panzer-Division in July 1941. From left to right, Hauptman Barth (Ib, supply officer), Model, Oberstleutnant Heinz Pomtow (Ia, operations officer), Major Oppen (IIa, personnel officer) and Leutnant Knesebeck (Ic, intelligence officer). Contrary to some post-war accounts, Model got along well with most of his staff members. (Author)

The Soviet winter counter-offensive began on 5 December, with the Kalinin Front's 29th and 31st Armies attacking AOK 9 at Kalinin while the Western Front attacked Panzergruppe 3 with the 1st Shock, 20th and 30th Armies. With his flanks caving in, Reinhardt was forced to conduct a fighting retreat back to Klin, while Model held off pursuit from the Western Front. Nevertheless, the Soviets briefly managed to encircle five of Reinhardt's motorized divisions, including Model's troops, in Klin by 14 December. It was only Soviet inexperience and desperate German counter-attacks that enabled these divisions to escape, but they were forced to abandon much of their artillery and vehicles. Model was perhaps the only German officer to enhance his reputation during the retreat from Moscow; while other senior officers were demanding further retreats, he actually protested orders to withdraw because of the inability of others to hold their sectors. Oftentimes he was out in the snow with his men, frequently with his pistol drawn to enforce crumbling discipline, moving from critical point to critical point, which earned him the nickname of 'Frontschwein' (front-line pig) from staff officers in the rear. Model was a pillar of strength during the retreat, demonstrating a talent for conducting tenacious rearguard actions that helped to prevent the German retreat from becoming a rout. Nevertheless, his corps suffered heavy losses from both the enemy and frostbite during the retreat from Moscow.

After further heavy fighting around Christmas, a brief lull settled across the Rzhev–Kalinin sector in early January 1942, which enabled both AOK 9 and Panzergruppe 3 to re-establish a tenuous line centreed on Rzhev. Generaloberst Adolf Strauß, commander of AOK 9, wanted to retreat farther because he expected the Soviet offensive to resume shortly, but Hitler forbade it. Sure enough, Colonel-General Ivan Konev massed 35 divisions in five armies in the Kalinin Front and resumed the offensive against AOK 9 on 8 January 1942. The Stavka's intent was to rip apart AOK 9 and Panzergruppe 3's front, then envelop Heeresgruppe Mitte from the north, while other Soviet armies enveloped it from the south, hopefully meeting around Vyazma. Konev pounded on AOK 9, which fought desperately to hold Rzhev, but the Soviet 39th Army achieved a major breakthrough on 10 January, tearing a wide gap through the sector held by SS-Standartenführer Hermann Fegelein's SS-Kavalleriebrigade. The next day, the Soviets pushed a mobile group with three cavalry divisions and a motorized division deep into AOK 9's rear areas, encircling three divisions of the VI Armeekorps at Olenino and reaching Strauß's headquarters in Sychevka. Staff officers and rear-area support personnel had to fight off Soviet tanks and infantry to prevent the fall of Sychevka and its vital railyard full of supplies. Strauß suffered a physical collapse, leaving AOK 9 leaderless. To make matters even worse, the Soviet Northwest Front achieved a major breakthrough near the boundary between Heeresgruppe Nord (Army Group North) and Heeresgruppe Mitte and encircled 90,000 troops of AOK 16 at Demyansk. The 4th Shock Army poured through the huge 260km-wide hole blown in the front and marched rapidly towards Smolensk and Vitebsk to sever Heeresgruppe Mitte's main supply lines. Looking at the imminent catastrophe, Generaloberst Franz Halder, the chief of the OKH, now called the Rhzev–Sychevka sector the 'most decisive spot on the Eastern Front'.

On 16 January, after two months as corps commander, Model was suddenly ordered to fly to the Führer's headquarters at Wolfsschanze (Wolf's Lair) in East Prussia, where he learned that he was being promoted to the rank of *Generaloberst* and replacing Strauß as commander of AOK 9. He was being entrusted with defeating the Soviet breakthrough and restoring the front. Model's stern demeanour made quite an impression on Hitler, who later said: 'Did you see that eye? I trust that man to do it, but I wouldn't want to serve under him.' Although Model was promoted ahead of many other more senior officers, few if any would have wanted to take command of a shattered and partly surrounded army. Yet Model took to this daunting task with his usual optimistic and energetic approach.

Model confers with Generaloberst Heinz Guderian, commander of Panzergruppe 2 during the initial stages of Operation *Barbarossa*. The two officers had enjoyed a cordial relationship since their days together in the Großer Generalstab and they continued to function well together throughout the war. (Author)

The final push towards Moscow left Panzergruppe 3 with long, exposed and vulnerable flanks, which the Red Army began to take advantage of on 5 December. Model found himself responsible for protecting these vital lines of communications. (Ian Barter)

THE HOUR OF DESTINY, 1942–45

Attack. Regain the initiative. Impose your will upon the enemy.
Model

Saving the northern flank

When Model arrived at AOK 9 headquarters in Sychevka, south of Rzhev, he found that his new command was in a complete shambles. On paper he had a dozen divisions, but after weeks of fighting and retreating most units had less than 25 per cent of their infantry left. The troops were exhausted, supplies were low and morale was crumbling. Even worse, three of the six divisions in VI Armeekorps were surrounded near Olenino, while the rest of the corps was holding onto Rzhev and the Volga line by their fingernails. Konev had pushed the bulk of his 29th and 39th Armies plus the 11th Cavalry Corps through a 14km-wide gap separating the Olenino Pocket from Rzhev, and by the time Model arrived some Soviet units were approaching the main German line of communication on the Minsk–Moscow highway. Inside his new headquarters, Model studied the situation map and then turned to his dispirited staff and informed them that AOK 9 would conduct a multi-division counter-attack within 72 hours to relieve the trapped forces at Olenino, thereby isolating the two encroaching Soviet armies. Although his staff protested about the impossibility of attacking with insufficient combat troops under brutal Arctic weather conditions with -40° C temperatures at night and a metre of snow on the ground, Model was adamant that AOK 9 would attack.

It was true that AOK 9's exhausted divisions were too depleted to conduct an attack on their own, but Heeresgruppe Mitte transferred units from 3. Panzerarmee (PzAOK 3) and 4. Armee (AOK 4) to protect its supply lines and Model worked with the OKH to arrange an extraordinary airlift of part of Infanterie-Regiment 337 from France to secure Sychevka. The most significant reinforcement was Generaloberst Heinrich von Viettinghoff-Scheel's

XLVI Armeekorps (mot.) with the SS-Division Reich and the 5. Panzer-Division. While Model was happy to receive these reinforcements, he was shocked to learn that the OKH wanted to direct how they were used. Because of increasing insubordination from his generals during the retreat from Moscow, Hitler began micro-managing important tactical operations and he ordered Model to use XLVI Armeekorps (mot.) in a local counter-attack at Gzhatsk rather than to relieve the Olenino Pocket. Upon hearing this Model flew back to Wolfsschanze and demanded an immediate audience with Hitler. When confronted, Hitler was adamant that Model follow orders, but Model stood his ground and openly demanded: 'Who commands the 9. Armee mein Führer, you or me?' Hitler was taken aback by this unheard of resistance by one of his generals, but not only did he concede Model's authority to use the reinforcements as he deemed appropriate, but he gained respect for the one general who did not kowtow before him.

A German machine-gun crew mans a portion of AOK 9's front line during the cruel winter of 1941–42. Although Model was committed to building a continuous front, oftentimes there was only sufficient manpower available to create a screen based around a few automatic weapons and forward observers. (Ian Barter)

Flying back to Sychevka, Model began his counter-offensive on schedule on the morning of 21 January, with VI Armeekorps launching pincer attacks from Olenino and Rzhev. It was not an impressive attack by Wehrmacht standards – only elements of two infantry divisions, four assault guns, some artillery and a few Luftwaffe sorties – but it occurred under the worst of weather conditions and with exhausted troops. After a week of desperate fighting, the counter-attack succeeded and not only re-established the link to the Olenino Pocket, but isolated nine Soviet divisions with 60,000 troops in the woods and swamps southwest of Rzhev. In order to mount this counter-attack, Model had been forced to ruthlessly strip other sectors around Rzhev of his remaining infantry and replace them with *Sperrverband* units (blocking units) and alarm battalions composed of clerks, convalescents, signalmen and artillerymen, which increased the risk of more Soviet penetrations. Indeed, the area south of Sychevka was virtually unprotected, which enabled the Soviet 18th Cavalry Division to reach the Moscow–Minsk Highway on 27 January and cut the main supply lines to AOK 9. With his hands full at Olenino, Model turned to Generalleutnant Erhard Raus, leading a small *Kampfgruppe* from the 6. Panzer-Division, restore the situation south of Sychevka. Raus succeeded brilliantly, using an extemporized armoured train and *Kampfgruppen* formed from mechanics and supply personnel to clear the Soviet cavalry off the rail lines, which cemented his relationship with the new army commander. As a senior commander, Model strove to develop a stable of subordinates he could trust to accomplish difficult missions, and Raus was one of the first to enter this group.

Konev was surprised by Model's ability to organize an effective counter-attack so swiftly, but he was not going to stand idly by and watch him smash the isolated 39th Army. He ordered his 29th Army to launch

an immediate attack to break through the narrow German corridor. Model anticipated this and moved some of his best troops to this sector, including Kampfgruppe Kumm, composed of the 650-man SS-Regiment Der Führer, four 88mm flak guns and five StuG III assault guns. Model ordered SS-Obersturmbannführer Otto Kumm to 'hold at all costs'. The Soviet 29th Army pounded on Kumm's *Kampfgruppe* for three weeks but failed to break through and suffered enormous losses in the

Soviet T-34 tanks from the Kalinin Front lead a Soviet attack into a forested area near Rzhev early in 1942. The Kalinin Front made repeated efforts to break through to the isolated AOK 29 and AOK 39, but failed. (Nik Cornish, AO 146)

process. Model kept close tabs on Kumm's defence, visiting frequently – even on horseback when snow blocked the road – and encouraging the troops to hold on. When it was over, Kumm had only 35 of his SS troops left, but he had accomplished his mission and Model personally decorated him with the Knight's Cross for his stubborn defence. Hitler was also quick to realize that Model had succeeded in reversing AOK 9's hopeless situation, so on 17 February he called him to the Wolfsschanze to receive the Knight's Cross with Oak Leaves.

As Konev's offensive ebbed in mid-February 1942, a stalemate developed and Model could turn to eliminate the isolated Soviet 39th Army and restore AOK 9's combat strength. In order to refill his depleted units, he pulled more support personnel from the rear and retrained them as infantrymen,

1   11 January: The Soviet 39th Army creates a breakthrough that isolates the German XXIII Armeekorps in Olenino while advancing south towards Sychevka

2   12–17 January: XXIII Armeekorps pulls its forces back into a hedgehog around Olenino, creating an 130km-wide gap between AOK 9 and AOK 16 to the west. The Soviet 22nd Army and 4th Shock Army advance into this gap.

3   18 January: Model arrives to take command of AOK 9 and shifts some units from the east side of the salient to build a new front between Rzhev and Sychevka. Hitler allows Model to use the 1. Panzer-Division and SS Reich Division from 3 PzAOK to stabilize the situation around Sychevka.

4   22–23 January: Model conducts a pincer attack with VI and XXIII Armeekorps, which re-establishes a link to the Olenino Pocket.

5   22 January: The Soviet 39th Army launches attacks against Sychevka and Ossuga, but Model's improvised defences hold.

6   25 January: Model orders Raus to guard the rail line south of Sychevka with his *Kampfgruppe* drawn from the 6. Panzer-Division and supply troops.

7   25 January: German reinforcements arrive by rail from France: the 246. Infanterie-Division is sent to occupy a critical road junction at Bely and another regiment of the 208. Infanterie-Division is sent to guard the main Smolensk–Vyazma rail line. The 403. Sicherungs-Division also helps to contain the 39th Army's advance.

8   26 January: Model sends Gruppe Recke (Infanterie-Regiment 169 and Kampfgruppe Kumm from SS Reich Division) to hold the vital Solomino sector.

9   27 January: The Soviet 11th Cavalry Corps temporarily cuts the Smolensk–Vyazma highway, severing the main supply line to three German armies, including AOK 9.

10   28 January: 4 PzAOK transfers XXXXVI Armeekorps with the 5. Panzer-Division to Model's AOK 9 for his counter-offensive.

11   1–15 February 1942: Konev makes repeated efforts to break through and reopen communications to the 39th Army, but Gruppe Recke's defence holds.

12   Late January to mid-February: The other armies in Zhukov's Western Front maintain continuous attacks against the eastern side of the Rzhev salient, which creates the risk of breakthroughs in other sectors.

13   1–5 February: Model launches his counter-offensive with XXXXVI Armeekorps, which slowly pushes northwest and splits the 29th Army from the 39th Army.

14   17 February: Reinforced with more armour and artillery, Model's final counter-attack crushes the trapped 29th Army, taking 5,000 prisoners.

Model stabilizes the AOK 9 front at Rzhev, January–February 1942

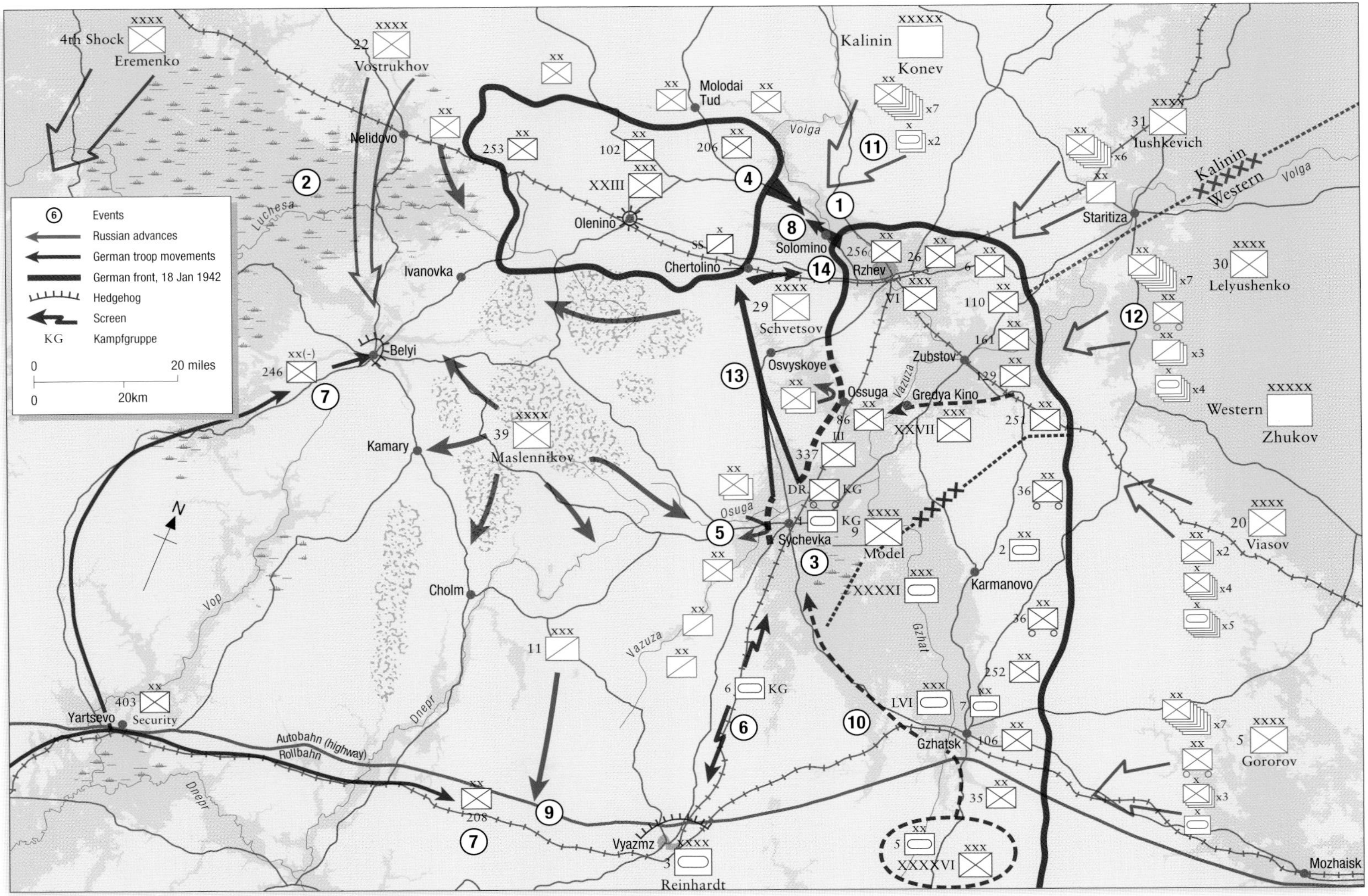

Map labels:

Mozhaisk, Kalinin, Western, Zhukov, Lelyushenko, 30, Viasov, 20, Gororov, 5, Starititza, 31, Iushkevich, x6, x7, x3, x4, 12, Konev, Kalinin, x7, x2, 11, 110, 251, 36, 2, Karmanovo, 36, 252, 106, 35, XXXXVI, Zubstov, Gredya Kino, XXVII, 5, Model, Osuga, Rzhev, 256, 26, 1, 14, 8, Solomino, Osuga, DR, KG, LVI, Gzhatsk, Gzhatsk, 10, 337, Svchevka, 3, 4, Molodai Tud, 206, Chertolino, Schvetsov, Osvyskoye, 29, 13, 5, 6 KG, 6, 102, XXIII, Olenino, 253, Maslennikov, 39, Vyazmz, Reinhardt, 9, Ivanovka, Belyi, Kamary, Cholm, 11, 7, 4th Shock, Eremenko, Vostrukhov, 22, Melidovo, 7, 246, 2, Yartsevo, Security, 403, Volga, Vazuza, Vazuza, Dnepr, Dnepr, Vop, Luchesa, Autobahn (highway), Rollbahn

Legend:

Events ⑥
Russian advances
German troop movements
German front, 18 Jan 1942
Hedgehog
Screen
KG Kampfgruppe

N

20 miles
20km
0   0

filling their duties with Russian auxiliaries. The few remaining tanks were concentrated, as was the artillery, to enable Model to direct them at the decisive point. Model put Raus in charge of reducing the 39th Army, which was dubbed the 'Snail Offensive' because AOK 9 had only enough resources to conduct small, set-piece attacks rather than continuous offensive operations. However, the isolated Soviet troops were also in dire straights, with limited ammunition and few heavy weapons left. Raus gradually pushed the 39th Army away from AOK 9's lines of communications, giving Model some elbowroom. By the time the Soviet Rzhev–Vyazma Offensive ended in mid-April 1942, Konev's Kalinin Front had suffered 341,000 casualties and AOK 9 had rebuilt a stable front line.

These leFH18 10.5cm howitzers are in firing positions about 3km behind the main line of resistance. AOK 9 originally had 660 artillery pieces of 10.5cm or larger at the start of Operation *Typhoon*, but many were abandoned during the retreat from Kalinin, leaving Model with barely 50 medium-artillery pieces to defend the Rzhev salient during the winter of 1941–42. (Ian Barter)

Model's defensive tactics

During the period of January–May 1942, Model began to introduce a series of tactical innovations and doctrinal changes that significantly improved AOK 9's ability to defeat Soviet offensives. Unlike the Panzer generals Reinhardt and Höpner, who seemed at a loss when they couldn't conduct proper *Bewegungskrieg* because of deep snow, mud and fuel shortages, Model learned to adapt and improvise with what he had. In order to gain some kind of force that could manoeuvre in snow and mud and independently from supplies of fuel, he stripped all the mounted reconnaissance troops from his infantry divisions and combined them to form a brigade-size Kavallerie-Kommando z.b.V. Turning to his depleted Panzer units, he directed the 5. Panzer-Division to form a ski battalion. Model also decided that rather than relying upon division and corps commanders to properly employ their remaining artillery assets, he would centralize fire planning under HArko 307 (Higher Artillery Command 307) – which ensured that Model had sufficient fire support where he needed it most. His most urgent need was to replace front-line infantry strength, which he did ruthlessly by ordering a 5 per cent reduction in headquarters and support troops, who were then promptly reassigned to infantry units. Because of heavy losses in vehicles and artillery during the retreat from Moscow, AOK 9 had a large number of unemployed artillerymen and mechanics, so Model also tapped these groups for infantry replacements. Needless to say, these measures were not popular in AOK 9, but they enabled Model to gradually rebuild a continuous front line.

During the retreat from Moscow, hard-pressed German units had been unable to utilize an elastic defence doctrine because of excessively wide fronts and insufficient troops, so they had developed an expediential strongpoint (*Stützpünkt*) defence based on fortified villages and towns.

However, Model was not in favour of this tactic since Soviet infantry could freely infiltrate into the gaps between strongpoints, and German positions in villages were vulnerable to artillery bombardment. Instead, Model decided to return to some of the methods proven on the Western Front in 1916–18, even though many Wehrmacht officers said that these tactics were not applicable on the Eastern Front. As a first step, Model put great emphasis on tactical intelligence gathering through infantry patrolling and he learned to listen to his Ic (intelligence officer). By gaining greater situational awareness, Model could anticipate the time and location of Soviet offensives and ensure that threatened sectors were reinforced. Secondly, he forced all his units to build a continuous front, even if it was very thin and manned only by support troops. It took Model six months to create a continuous front in the Rzhev salient, but it paid dividends against the next two Soviet offensives. By ensuring that there were no gaps in his front, Model based his defence on forward observers connected by field phones eventually up to HArko 307, which could mass artillery fire to break up Soviet infantry attacks before they broke his lines. Thirdly, despite Hitler's orders against preparing 'fall-back' positions, Model always hedged his bets by quietly preparing fortified 'switch' lines in his rear that troops could occupy in the event of a Soviet breakthrough.

The heart of Model's defensive tactics lay in effective forward observers who could call in devastating artillery barrages to break up Soviet infantry attacks, enabling Panzerjäger tank-destroyers to pick off the unsupported T-34s. (Bundesarchiv, Bild 101I-198-1363-29A, Fotograf: Henisch)

The Rzhev meatgrinder

Throughout the 'Snail Offensive' Model demonstrated his characteristic restless energy, flying from one divisional command post to the next. While returning from an inspection trip over the critical Belyi sector on 23 May 1942, Model's Fiesler Storch was flying about 50m over the forest when it was fired upon by a Soviet machine gunner. Both Model and his pilot were hit. One round struck Model in his hip, passed through his chest and then exited from his shoulder. Model was gravely wounded and it was only the ability of his wounded pilot to land the damaged aircraft at a nearby German field hospital that saved his life. Model's condition was critical for several days, but once he stabilized he was sent home to recuperate in Dresden. During Model's absence Generaloberst Viettinghoff took over temporary command of AOK 9.

Model spent 11 weeks recuperating from his wounds. While he was away, Viettinghoff conducted Operation *Seydlitz* from 2–12 July, which finally closed the Belyi gap and destroyed the trapped 39th Army. Model's cavalry brigade performed particularly well, manoeuvring through the swampy forests. However, the Stavka was still

intent upon crushing the Rzhev salient and sent significant reinforcements to Konev to rebuild the Kalinin Front for another major offensive. Konev attacked with two armies in an attempt to capture Rzhev on 30 July, while Zhukov arrived to take personal command of the Western Front and attacked with two more armies on 4 August. The four Soviet armies slowly pushed Viettinghoff's troops back 32km and made a significant bulge in the northeast corner of the Rzhev salient. However, Zhukov failed to achieve a major breakthrough. Back in Dresden, Model was impatient to return to his command and flew to Sychevka on 7 August. By the time he arrived back at the front, Zhukov's offensive was beginning to wane, having failed to take Rzhev, and Model set about restoring AOK 9's bruised front line.

Zhukov believed that AOK 9 was almost broken and he still cherished dreams of crushing the Rzhev salient with a pincer attack. Konev was shifted to take command of the Western Front, while Colonel-General Maksim Purkaev took over the Kalinin Front. Zhukov remained as Stavka coordinator for both fronts, which made him overall commander. In conjunction with the Stavka, Zhukov planned Oparation *Mars* to cut off the Rzhev salient, just as the Don and Stalingrad Fronts conducted Operation *Uranus* to encircle AOK 6 in Stalingrad. Zhukov's concept for Operation *Mars* was straightforward: Kalinin Front's 41st Army would attack AOK 9 on the western side of the salient while 20th Army would attack the eastern side, and after breakthroughs were achieved their armoured spearheads would then link up and complete the encirclement of Model's army.

Four weeks before Operation *Mars* began, Model's intelligence officer, Oberst Georg Buntrock, accurately assessed that the Soviet Kalinin and Western Fronts would soon conduct a massive pincer offensive to cut off AOK 9 in the Rzhev salient. Based upon radio intercepts, aerial reconnaissance and

25–28 November 1942

1 Operation *Mars* begins with the Soviet 20th Army attacking along the river Vazuza. Although the supporting flank attacks fail, the 8th Guards Corps achieves a small breakthrough and Konev pushes the 2nd Guards Cavalry Corps and the 6th Tank Corps into the breach.

2 The Soviet 41st Army achieves a breakthrough against a section of the Bely sector, held by a Luftwaffe division. Purkaev commits the 1st Mechanized Corps into the breach and it advances 35km.

3 Zhukov's intent is for 20th and 41st Armies' mobile groups to link up west of Sychevka.

4 The Soviet 22nd Army also achieves a significant breakthrough in the Luchesa River valley. Harpe's XXXXI Panzerkorps faces a double envelopment.

5 As a supporting attack, the Soviet 39th Army attacks the German XXIII Armeekorps and slowly pushes it back several kilometers.

6 Model requests the 12., 19. and 20. Panzer-Divisionen from Heeresgruppe Mitte's reserve, which will be commanded by XXX Armeekorps.

7 The 1. Panzer-Division delays the 1st Mechanized Corps and prevents Bely from becoming encircled.

8 The Soviet 41st Army makes repeated attacks on the Germans in Bely but fails to capture the town.

9 The Soviet 20th Army's attack becomes stalled after a 12km penetration. All efforts to widen the breach fail. Commitment of the 5th Tank Corps fails to budge Arnim's defence.

29–30 November 1942

10 Arnim counter-attacks with the 5. and 9. Panzer-Divisionen, cutting off the 6th Tank Corps and 2nd Guards Cavalry Corps. Both Soviet formations are gradually crushed.

11 Model orders the Grossdeutschland Division to block the Soviet 3rd Mechanized Corps.

1–9 December 1942

12 Fretter-Pico's XXX Armeekorps counter-attacks into the flank of the 41st Army and quickly isolates the 6th Rifle Corps and 1st Mechanized Corps. Both Soviet corps are crushed.

10–20 December 1942

13 In mop-up operations, the 12. Panzer-Division is sent to regain ground in the Luchesa valley.

Defence of the Rzhev salient, 25 November to 15 December 1942

Legend

- ⑥ Events
- Soviet advances
- Maximum Soviet advance
- German troop movements
- Front line 25 Nov 1942

XXXXX Purkaev

0 — 20 km
0 — 20 miles

N

Place and unit labels:

Mozhaisk, Cherevichenko, Starititsa, Polenov, 31, x10, Western Konev, Kolpakchi, 30, x9, Kiriukhin, 20, Zhuravlev, 29, x4, x4, x7, 3 GD, Karmanovo, 342, 2, VIII, Gzhatsk, Von Esebeck, Reinhardt, 3, Vyazma, Zubtsov, Gredya, Kino, 3, GD, 2 GD, 1, 8 GD, 6, 5, Ossuga, 337, Rzhev, 87, 87, 256, 129, 95, 102, 2 GD CAV, 78, Model, 9, Solomino, Weiss, XXVII, Oswyskoye, Chertolino, Von Arnim, XXX VIII, AOK 9, PzAOK 3, Zygin, 135, 158, 373, 28, 81, 39, 206, 186, GD, XXIII, Hilpert, 14, 29, Molodai Tud, Olenino, 253, 110, Kalinin, Nelidovo, Purkaev, 155, 362, 185, Katukov, 3, 218, 93, 86, 246, GD, III, XXXXI, Harpe, Ivanovka, Belyi, Kamary, Cholm, 1, 12, 6, Dnepr, Tarasov, Solomatin, 2, 17 GD, 41, 22, Iushkevich, Luchesa, LFD, 19, 20, Fretter-Pico, SS, Volga, Reserves, Yartsevo, Vop, Osuga, Vazuza, Dnepr, Autobahn (highway), Rollbahn, Sychevka

Event markers: ① ② ③ ④ ⑤ ⑥ ⑦ ⑧ ⑨ ⑩ ⑪ ⑫ ⑬

prisoner interrogations, Buntrock was able to specify the likely Soviet attack sectors. For once, German intelligence not only got it right, but they had a commander who heeded its warning. Model began heavily reinforcing the threatened sectors. In particular, he formed a double line of bunkers and fighting positions, laid more mines and cut down trees to clear fields of fire in the vital river Vazuza sector held by General der Panzertruppen Jurgen von Arnim's XXXIX Panzerkorps. During this time, Model visited the critical sectors on a daily basis, sometimes on a tracked Kettenkrad to make it through the snow, and personally ensured that his defences were ready. Model also positioned the 5. and 9. Panzer-Divisionen to counter-attack any breakthrough in Arnim's sector and the 1. Panzer-Division to support the west side of the salient. None of these Panzer divisions had been fully rebuilt since their battering in the winter of 1941–42 and they had a total of only 157 tanks between them, but fuel and ammunition were sufficient. AOK 9's infantry units were equally depleted, with battalion strength averaging 50 per cent, but by November 1942 they were mostly hardened veterans and occupied stoutly built defensive positions. HArko 307 controlled about 260 medium artillery pieces and, thanks to Model's prior planning, it had established pre-planned engagement areas in all the critical sectors. Thus, thanks to poor Soviet operational security procedures, Model gained weeks to prepare his defence and was able to develop contingency plans with Generalfeldmarschall Günther von Kluge to receive up to three more Panzer divisions from elsewhere in Heeresgruppe Mitte if needed.

Operation *Mars* began on the morning of 25 November 1942 with four simultaneous assaults around the periphery of the Rzhev salient. Zhukov committed over 800,000 assault troops and 2,000 tanks to crush AOK 9. Zhukov's main effort, made by Konev's Western Front, was the 20th Army attack on Arnim's XXXIX Panzerkorps on the river Vazuza on the eastern side of the salient. Despite massing 53 regiments of artillery on this narrow sector, snow and fog severely degraded the 90-minute Soviet artillery preparation and the intact German infantry positions repulsed three rifle divisions with 50 per cent losses. However, Konev – egged on by Zhukov – continued to launch wave after wave of infantry attacks into the 'Rzhev meatgrinder' until finally a small breakthrough was achieved. Konev then prematurely committed his mobile group – the 6th Tank Corps and the 2nd Guard Cavalry Corps – to push through the gap, leading to a chaotic traffic jam and a target-rich environment for Model's centralized artillery. When the Luftwaffe provided some Stuka sorties to support AOK 9, Model directed them at Konev's armoured traffic jam and they wreaked great havoc. Konev's mobile forces managed

Generalleutnant Hans Krebs (1898–1945), was Model's chief of staff at AOK 9 from 1942–43, then at Heeresgruppe Mitte in 1944 and finally at Heeresgruppe B. Krebs spoke fluent Russian and had a good grasp of Russian military methods, but lacked the flamboyance of Model, which made him ideal as a chief of staff. (Bundesarchiv, Bild 146-1978-111-10A)

to push 12km westward and cut the Sychevka–Rzhev railway line, but he was unable to widen the 20th Army's breach in the German front and his best forces were soon strung out in a thin salient. Arnim conducted a brilliant tactical defence and then counter-attacked on 29 November with the 5. and 9. Panzer-Divisionen, which cut off Konev's mobile group and destroyed it in a classic *Kessel* battle.

Purkaev's Kalinin Front attacked the Rzhev salient at three places: two major attacks on the west side by the 22nd and 41st Armies against General der Panzertruppen Josef Harpe's XXXXI Panzerkorps and a supporting attack in the north by the 39th Army against XXIII Armeekorps. The 41st Army scored a major breakthrough south of Belyi by blasting a hole through the weak 2. Luftwaffen-Feld-Division and then pushing the 1st Mechanized Corps and the 6th Rifle Corps through to advance 35km eastward to the river Nacha before being blocked by the 1. Panzer-Division. At the same time, the 22nd Army tore a substantial gap in the northern part of Harpe's front in the Luchesa Valley and then pushed the 3rd Mechanized Corps through. Harpe's entire corps was clearly on the verge of collapse from these two penetrations. In the north, the 39th Army made slow but steady gains.

Model's best subordinate commander for much of 1942–45 was General Josef Harpe (1887–1968). Harpe served him well as commander of XXXXI Armeekorps (mot.) at Rzhev and Kursk, then took over AOK 9 from Model in November 1943 and fought under him in Poland and northern Ukraine. (Bundesarchiv, Bild 146-1981-104-30, Fotograf: Heinrich Hoffmann)

Model was faced with four simultaneous enemy offensives around the perimeter of his army, but he was able to quickly assess which threats were the most dangerous and send just enough forces to shore up the local defences while assembling his armour for counter-attacks. Arnim already had his sector in hand by 30 November, but the situation in Harpe's sector grew worse as the two Soviet mechanized corps continued to drive eastwards, and Model requested Kluge to send the 12., 19. and 20. Panzer-Divisionen from army-group reserves. Kluge agreed, but it would take days for them to arrive and Model was forced to fight a desperate holding action in the west until the Panzers arrived. Harpe's troops conducted an incredible defence of Belyi, which prevented the two Soviet attacking armies from joining up and which left both their mechanized spearheads at the end of long, exposed salients.

By early December the Soviet attacks had stalled because of German resistance, heavy losses and the difficulty of keeping their spearheads in supply. At this point, Model unleashed the 19. and 20. Panzer-Divisionen into the flank of the 41st Army's long salient south of Belyi, and by 9 December its spearhead had been surrounded in another *Kessel*. Both the 1st Mechanized Corps and the 6th Rifle Corps were utterly smashed in a week-long battle of annihilation. Meanwhile, Harpe used the 'Großdeutschland' Division to seal off the 3rd Mechanized Corps' penetration.

Ironically, only the supporting attack by the 39th Army in the north achieved any lasting success, by forcing XXIII Armeekorps to pull back a few kilometers. By 20 December, even Zhukov had to concede that Operation *Mars* had failed and he called off the offensive. AOK 9's lines – as well as its spirit – had bent, but not broken.

Model's defeat of Operation *Mars* was one of the great accomplishments of his career and one of the most impressive defensive victories of World War II. If Zhukov had crushed AOK 9 in the Rzhev salient, at the same time that AOK 6 was encircled at Stalingrad, the entire German front in the east could easily have collapsed in the winter of 1942–43. Instead, Soviet losses during Operation *Mars* were catastrophic: approximately 100,000 dead and 235,000 wounded, or 40 per cent of the forces committed. Armour losses were nearly 85 per cent, with the Germans claiming 1,852 tanks destroyed. Six elite Soviet corps (1MC, 3MC, 5TC, 6TC, 2GCC and 6RC) were either destroyed or crippled. AOK 9's losses were significant, but all of its units remained combat effective. However, it is important to note that Model's victory was based upon the availability of six Panzer divisions, which were in increasingly short supply. Despite the battering inflicted on both Soviet fronts, Model still needed 30 divisions to hold the Rzhev salient, which was a luxury that the Ostheer

The Rzhev meatgrinder: Kampfgruppe Stieber repulses Soviet wave attacks during Operation *Mars*, 25 November 1942

Kampfgruppe Stieber, consisting of the II/Panzergrenadier Regiment 14 (from the 5. Panzer-Division) under Major Kurt Stieber, was assigned to defend the fortified village of Grediakino. When the Soviet 20th Army began Operation *Mars* on the morning of 25 November 1942 it was soon apparent that Stieber occupied a key position in the centre of the enemy's intended axis of advance. Model ordered Stieber to hold Grediakino at all costs, in order to restrict the Soviets to a narrow breach in AOK 9's continuous front. Stieber's defences consisted of several stoutly constructed bunkers and pillboxes arrayed around the village and connected by communication trenches. After a punishing artillery penetration, the Soviet 42nd Guards Rifle Division and 93rd Tank Brigade attacked Grediakino. Stieber's men repulsed the first attack and destroyed ten tanks, but the 20th Army committed more armour and infantry to this sector and began a series of relentless attacks. Late in the afternoon, the 25th Tank Brigade and some Soviet infantry broke into the western edge of the village and had to be defeated in close combat. Here, German Panzerjägers (**1**) engage a KV-1 tank (**2**) with the brand-new Haft-Hohlladung magnetic anti-tank mine, while a MG-42 team (**3**) pins down the supporting Soviet infantry (**4**). A forward observer with a field telephone (**5**) calls down 81mm mortar fire. Stieber succeeded in repulsing this assault as well, but Grediakino was surrounded by nightfall. Nevertheless, Stieber held Grediakino for six days until his battalion was reduced from about 300 troops down to only 119 effectives, and virtually out of ammunition. He then abandoned Grediakino and escaped through Soviet lines to rejoin German units on the Vazuza. Throughout the siege, Model was able to sustain Stieber's beleaguered defence with timely aerial resupply drops and artillery support. Ultimately, Operation *Mars* failed because of the Soviet inability to quickly overcome intact German defensive positions.

(Eastern Army) could no longer afford after the defeat at Stalingrad.

Although Hitler had refused to abandon the Rzhev salient throughout 1942, after Model's impressive victory he was more willing to listen to his recommendations. Hitler was particularly swayed by Model's argument that evacuation would free eight divisions for OKH to create a small reserve. Model argued that the creation of a centrally controlled 'European reserve' could give the Wehrmacht the ability to better respond to crises, but Hitler ignored him and decided that the reserve should be used to mount a new summer offensive. On 6 February 1943 Hitler authorized Model to evacuate the salient. Model's staff developed Operation *Büffel* (Buffalo) to conduct the evacuation in a series of phased withdrawals. Unlike Zhukov, Model placed a tight veil of security over the evacuation preparations, so the Soviets were unaware of the withdrawal until it actually began on 1 March. AOK 9 abandoned Rzhev on 3 March and Sychevka five days later, falling back to new phase lines every few days. Once they detected the German withdrawal, Konev and Purkaev initiated a hasty pursuit but German rearguards inflicted heavy casualties upon them. Model's losses in the retreat were minor, and once the evacuation was complete his army was shifted from the left flank of Heeresgruppe Mitte to its right flank, in the Orel salient.

Model was quick to recognize heroism among his troops during the successful defence against Operation *Mars*. Here, on 12 December 1942, he (centre) awards the Knight's Cross to Generalleutnant Paul Völckers, commander of the 78. Infanterie-Division. Standing to the right of Model with a bandaged head is Oberwachtmeister Fritz Amling, who had been awarded the Knight's Cross the day before. (Nik Cornish, WH 922)

Operation *Zitadelle*, April–July 1943

After Generalfeldmarschall Erich von Manstein, commander of Heeresgruppe Süd, recaptured Kharkov on 14 March 1943, a strange lull settled over the Eastern Front. Model, like most German senior commanders, wanted to remain on the defensive and rebuild his forces so that they could defeat the inevitable Soviet offensives. However, Manstein was in an aggressive mood after his own victory at Kharkov and pressed Hitler and the OKH for an offensive to cut off the Soviet Central and Voronezh Fronts in the Kursk salient as soon as the spring weather permitted. Hitler became convinced that the Wehrmacht needed a significant operational victory in the East in 1943 in order to retain the strategic initiative as well as to restore the German people's confidence in ultimate victory after the Stalingrad catastrophe. He believed that using Model's AOK 9 in the Orel salient and Manstein's 4. Panzerarmee (PzAOK 4) around Kharkov to conduct a classic pincer attack against the 180km-wide base of the Kursk salient could encircle and destroy eight Soviet armies, which would give Germany a valuable respite.

As Generaloberst Kurt Zeitzler, chief of staff of the OKH, began to refine Manstein's enthusiastic concept into Operation *Zitadelle*, Model was notably less sanguine about the prospects for offensive success. AOK 9 was in poor condition for a large-scale offensive, with its infantry divisions at only 60 per cent or less of authorized strength, as well as having significantly less armour and artillery than PzAOK 4. Even if he received substantial reinforcements, Model did not like the idea of a frontal assault into the teeth of a strong Soviet defence and told Zeitzler that the offensive would bring 'only large losses and no success'. Model joined with Guderian in labeling *Zitadelle* as 'senseless' and sent a detailed memorandum outlining his argument to the OKH in late April. Since Hitler himself was reconsidering the wisdom of *Zitadelle*, he seized upon Model's memorandum to justify a postponement. Yet instead of heeding Model's warning and cancelling *Zitadelle*, Hitler decided merely to wait until both AOK 9 and PzAOK 4 were reinforced with more troops and tanks, particularly the new Tigers and Panthers. Operation *Zitadelle* was postponed four more times, as both sides poured additional resources into the area for the decisive battle. While Model's AOK 9 received no Panthers and only a single battalion of Tigers, it was able to stockpile 9,174 tons of fuel and 12,300 tons of ammunition; at least Model's Panzers would not be handicapped by insufficient fuel as the German offensives had been in 1941–42. Finally, Hitler set the start date for Operation *Zitadelle* as 5 July.

At the start of Operation *Zitadelle*, Model's AOK 9 was reinforced to 21 divisions, including six Panzer divisions, by stripping the rest of Kluge's Heeresgruppe Mitte of armour and artillery. In addition to the Tiger battalion, the OKH sent Model two battalions of Ferdinand tank destroyers and a battalion of SturmPanzer IVs. With these reinforcements, Model's AOK 9 was expected to attack Konstantin Rokossovsky's Central Front on the northern part of the Kursk salient, penetrate three lines of defence, and then link up with Manstein's forces near Kursk. Despite his misgivings, Model concentrated ten of his divisions and almost 1,000 tanks against a narrow 19km-wide penetration corridor occupied by General Nikolai P. Pukhov's 13th Army, which had two rifle divisions in the first line of defence and two more in the second. Model designated General der Panzertruppen Joachim Lemelsen's XLVII Panzerkorps as his main effort (*Schwerpunkt*) and Harpe's XXXXI Panzerkorps as the supporting effort. The XXIII Armeekorps and XXXXVI Panzerkorps would make smaller supporting attacks with infantry on AOK 9's flanks, but their primary intent was to divert Rokossovsky's attention from the real *Schwerpunkt* in the centre. Thanks to his active battlefield reconnaissance efforts, Model was well aware that the Soviet 13th Army had laid over 5,000 mines

A German reconnaissance unit mounted in Sd. Kfz. 251 personnel carriers cautiously probes towards the outskirts of a burning Russian village during Operation *Zitadelle*. Although the flat tabletop steppe appeared to offer excellent potential for rapid mechanized advance, the depth and ferocity of the Soviet defence limited German movements to a grinding crawl. (Ian Barter)

German infantry approach the smoldering remains of a Soviet tank platoon during the early stages of AOK 9's offensive in July 1943. Rokossovsky's premature commitment of his 2nd Tank Army cost him about half his available armour, but succeeded in preventing Model from penetrating the Soviet second line of defence. (Ian Barter)

per mile (1.6km) of front and had built a formidable anti-tank defence in depth. So, unlike Manstein, he decided to use only one Panzer division on the first day of the offensive and to rely on his heavy armour, artillery and engineers to create gaps in the Soviet defensive belts that his Panzers could then exploit. Model was also more conservative than Manstein in planning his part of *Zitadelle*, because he realized that the 2. Panzerarmee (PzAOK 2) held the 250km-long northern part of the Orel salient with only 17 divisions. Opposing this thin defence, the Soviet Western and Bryansk Fronts had a four-to-one superiority in both manpower and armour, which they could use to strike Model's rear while he was preoccupied with *Zitadelle*. Consequently, Model wanted to keep as much of his armour in reserve as possible in order to respond to Soviet actions. Furthermore, he quietly began laying out the Hagen Stellung (Hagen Line) across the base of the Orel salient – against Hitler's direct order not to build rearward defences – so that AOK 9 would have prepared positions to fall back upon if necessary.

After a rainy night, which turned the battlefield into a muddy morass, Operation *Zitadelle* began at 0430hrs on 5 July with Model's artillery pounding the Soviet 13th Army positions with an 80-minute bombardment. His primary tactical objective was to seize the high ground south of the village of Ol'khovatka, which would provide the necessary jump-off point to reach Kursk 70km to the south. Lemelsen's corps, using only the 6. Infanterie-Division, 20. Panzer-Division and the Tiger battalion, succeeded in penetrating 5km through the 15th Rifle Division's first line of defence in less than four hours, but was then stopped short of the second line of defence. On their left, Harpe's corps, using two infantry divisions, the Ferdinands and the SturmPanzers, made a significant dent in the 81st Rifle Division's defence north of Ponyri. Effective close air support from Luftflotte 6 was critical in assisting the advance of Model's *Schwerpunkt* through the dense Soviet defences. By the end of the first day of the offensive Model's forces had gouged out a penetration 15km wide and up to 8km deep at a cost of over 7,000 casualties, but no breakthroughs had been achieved. During the course of the day, Model was in constant motion, visiting each corps headquarters to get the tactical picture in its sector, redirecting engineer units to clear previously undetected minefields and directing his artillery and Luftwaffe assets against centres of Soviet resistance.

The critical command decision facing Model as army commander was gauging the correct time and place to commit his armoured reserves. Aware that the 29th Rifle Corps' two front-line divisions and a tank brigade had been badly mauled on the first day, Model began cautiously committing his armour on 6 July, feeding the 2., 9. and 18. Panzer-Divisionen into the fight in order to help breach Pukhov's second line of defence. At this point Rokossovsky made an important tactical mistake by committing his main armour reserve – the 456 tanks of Lieutenant-General Aleksei G. Rodin's 2nd Tank Army – prematurely, piecemeal and straight into Model's *Schwerpunkt*. A huge tank battle began in the rolling terrain west of Ponyri on the edge of the Soviet second defensive belt. By nightfall on the second day, the commitment of the 2nd Tank Army delayed Model's attack against Pukhov's second line of defence for 24 hours, but it resulted in much of Rokossovsky's armour being dispersed and unavailable for a concentrated counter-attack.

Sensing the fleeting opportunity, Model ordered Harpe to launch a major three-division assault against Ponyri on 7 July, but the heavily reinforced 307th Rifle Division managed to hold on to the village. Meanwhile, Lemelsen continued to push towards Ol'khovatka with three Panzer divisions, but the 17th Guards Rifle Corps limited his advance to only 2–3km. Rokossovsky continued to feed reserves into the battle whenever the Germans showed signs of local success and the battle devolved into an attritional slugfest that could have only one result for the outnumbered Germans. Model committed his last reserves, the 4. Panzer-Division, on 8 July, but his advance was stopped cold by an impenetrable wall of Soviet tanks, infantry, artillery and mines. After two more days of diminishing combat, Model realized that his part of the offensive had failed and he shifted his forces to a defensive posture. Three days later Hitler cancelled Operation *Zitadelle*.

Model's forces suffered 20,720 casualties during the seven-day offensive, including 4,567 killed or missing (about 6 per cent of AOK 9's total strength). In terms of equipment, AOK 9 lost 88 tanks and assault guns destroyed along with about 250 more damaged. Nevertheless, Model still had considerable combat power left in AOK 9, including six relatively intact Panzer divisions and six infantry divisions. In contrast, Rokossovsky's Central Front suffered 33,897 casualties, including 15,336 killed (about 10 per cent of his forces committed). Soviet armour losses in this sector were 526 tanks out of 1,029 committed. Model failed to achieve his operational objectives of inflicting disproportionate losses on the enemy or seizing key terrain. However, his AOK 9 was in far better shape than Manstein's Heeresgruppe Süd to deal with the Soviet counter-offensives, which they knew were sure to follow the failure of Operation *Zitadelle*.

German troops cautiously enter the edge of a village behind a StuG III assault gun. During Operation *Zitadelle*, Model tried to conserve his armour and relied upon infantry and assault gun units to clear out villages. (Ian Barter)

Holding off Operation *Kutuzov*, July–August 1943

While waiting for Operation *Zitadelle* in the spring, the Soviet Stavka had ordered the Bryansk, Western and Central Fronts to prepare Operation *Kutuzov*, a counter-offensive to eliminate the German-held Orel salient, which was to

commence as soon as the German offensive was defeated. Now that *Zitadelle* had failed and AOK 9 presumably crippled, the Stavka ordered the Bryansk and Western Fronts to begin Operation *Kutuzov* by attacking PzAOK 2 on the northern flank of the Orel salient. This formation had been stripped of armour and artillery in order to strengthen AOK 9 for Operation *Zitadelle*, and had almost no reserves. Against this weakened PzAOK 2, the Soviet Western Front massed

General der Panzertruppen Joachim Lemelsen's XLVII Panzerkorps advanced southward towards the village of Ol'khovatka with three Panzer divisions on the morning of 6 July 1943, but could not budge the tough 17th Guards Rifle Corps. For the first time, a German armoured *Schwerpunkt* was stopped cold. (Ian Barter)

the 11th Guards Army, which had a dozen full-strength rifle divisions and three artillery divisions. The Stavka anticipated that the spearheads of the Western and Bryansk Fronts would reach Orel within 48 hours and precipitate a collapse of the salient.

The first day of the Soviet offensive began spectacularly on the morning of 12 July, with the 11th Guards Army smashing through a weak sector near Ul'ianovo with six rifle divisions, then committing two tank corps to advance 10km into the German rear. The situation grew worse on 13 July as the Soviets committed more forces and continued to advance. Model spent two days demanding that he be given command authority over PzAOK 2, which was not granted until 14 July. In desperation, Hitler finally placed Model in command of PzAOK 2 as well as his own AOK 9 and ordered him to restore the front line. This was a sound military decision, based upon

1   12 July: Operation *Kutuzov* begins with the Western Front's 11th Guards Army attacking PzAOK 2's LIII Armeekorps. Bagramian masses nine rifle divisions and an artillery corps against the German 293. Infanterie-Division near Ul'ianovo and smashes through the German front. He then commits the 1st and 5th Tank Corps into the penetration corridor and they begin fanning out.
2   13 July: PzAOK 2 is unable to seal off the breakthrough with the 5. Panzer-Division but prevents further Soviet advance westward.
3   13 July: The Bryansk Front attacks Rendulic's XXXV Armeekorps with three rifle divisions from the 3rd Army and six rifle divisions from 63rd Army. Rendulic conducts a very skilful defence that limits the advance.
4   14 July: Hitler places Model in command of PzAOK 2 as well as his own AOK 9. Model quickly begins redeploying Harpe's XXXXI Panzerkorps to contain the breakthrough by the 11th Guards Army, as well as sending the 2. and 8. Panzer-Divisionen to reinforce Rendulic's XXXV Armeekorps. Model assigns Harpe to command the forces on the northern side of the salient, Rendulic to command those in the east and Lemelsen those in the south.
5   15 July: Stalin orders Rokossovsky's Central Front to join the offensive, but his forces are still too depleted from the fighting around Ponyri, so AOK 9 has little difficulty fending off initial attacks by the 13th and 48th Armies.
6   19 July: The Bryansk Front commits the 700 tanks of General-Lieutenant Rybalko's 3rd Guards Tank Army against XXXV Armeekorps, but Model has built a very strong defence east of Orel with three Panzer divisions, which stops Rybalko's tanks.
7   21 July: Model shifts XXIII Armeekorps to seal the gap between LV Armeekorps and Gruppe Harpe.
8   21–25 July: Rybalko's 3rd Guards Tank Army is shifted south and supports a new offensive by 13th and 48th Armies, which gradually begins rolling up Lemelsen's XLVII Panzerkorps, which now only has infantry divisions. Zmiyevka is captured.
9   26 July: Badanov's 4th Tank Army (containing 500 tanks) joins the battle, which forces Gruppe Harpe to evacuate Bolkhov.
10   31 July: Hitler finally authorizes a withdrawal from the Orel salient. On 1 August Operation *Herbstreise* begins, with both PzAOK 2 and AOK 9 gradually falling back towards the Hagen Stellung.
11   4 August: Rokossovsky's 70th Army and 2nd Tank Army join the attack against the south side of the Orel salient, which bends back Model's right flank.
12   5 August: Orel is evacuated and falls to the Soviets.
13   18 August: The Operation *Kutuzov* offensive comes to a halt short of the Hagen Stellung.

Model's defence of the Orel salient, 18 August to 26 September 1944

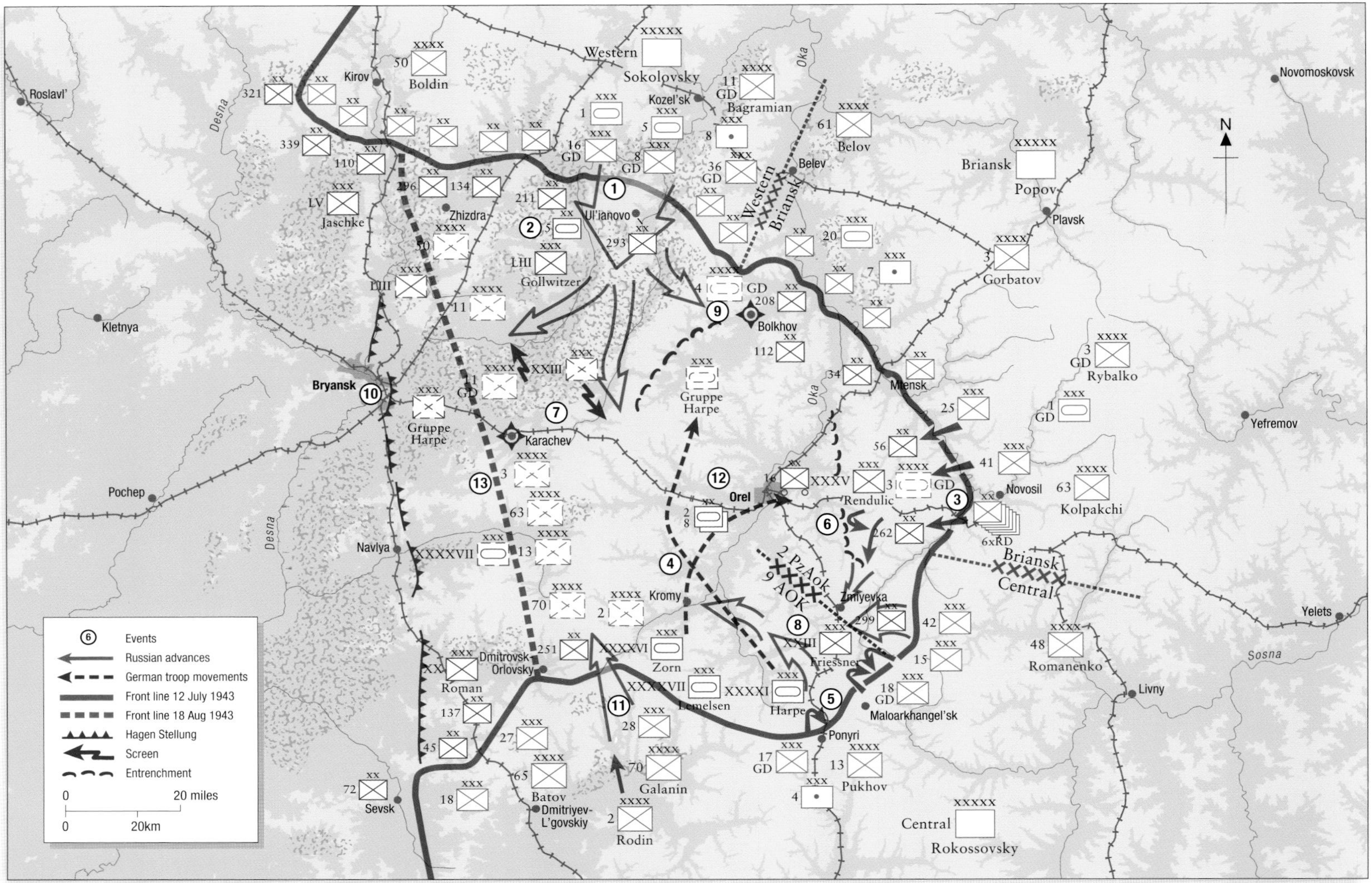

Legend:

Events ⑥

Russian advances

German troop movements

Front line 12 July 1943

Front line 18 Aug 1943

Hagen Stellung

Screen

Entrenchment

0 — 20 miles
0 — 20km

Selected map labels:

Novomoskovsk, Yefremov, Yelets, Roslavl', Kletnya, Pochep, Livny, Romanenko, Rokossovsky, Central, Pukhov, Galanin, Dmitriyev-L'govsky, Sevsk, Naviya, Bryansk, Kirov, Boldin, Jaschke, Zhizdra, Sokolovsky, Kozel'sk, Western, Belov, Bagramian, Belev, Gorbatov, Popov, Briansk, Plavsk, Rybalko, Kolpakchi, Novosil, Mtsensk, Rendulic, Zmiyevka, Maloarkhangel'sk, Ponyri, Orel, Bolkhov, Gruppe Harpe, Kromy, Zorn, Harpe, Trogelsen, Batov, Rodin, Roman, Dmitrovsk-Orlovsky, Karachev, Gollwitzer, Ullanovo

Briansk Central, Western Briansk, 2 PzAOK, 9 AOK, Gruppe Harpe

Events numbered ① ② ③ ④ ⑤ ⑥ ⑦ ⑧ ⑨ ⑩ ⑪ ⑫ ⑬

Only two days after AOK 9 suspended its offensive, the Soviets began Operation *Kutuzov* to eliminate the Orel salient. Model used the advantage of interior lines to shift Ferdinand tank destroyers and 88mm guns to stiffen Generalmajor Lothar Rendulic's XXXV Armeekorps in the eastern part of the salient. (Ian Barter)

the principle of unity of command, and it put Model in charge of the defence of the entire Orel salient, while the enemy had three different front commanders tasked to conduct Operation *Kutuzov*. Model quickly began redeploying three of his Panzer divisions under Harpe to contain the breakthrough by 11th Guards Army, as well as sending some reinforcements to Generalmajor Lothar Rendulic, commander of XXXV Armeekorps, which was holding off the Bryansk Front on the eastern side of the salient. Rendulic conducted a skilful defence with limited resources and repulsed the initial attacks by Bryansk Front, earning praise from Model. Stalin ordered Rokossovsky to join the offensive with his Central Front on 15 July, but his forces were still too depleted from the fighting around Ponyri, so AOK 9 had little difficulty fending off Rokossovsky's tentative jabs.

By mid-July, Model had his hands full, commanding 37 German divisions with 475,000 troops and 825 tanks while fending off concentric attacks by three Soviet fronts that had over 1.2 million troops and 2,800 tanks. Rather than use standard corps organization, he tasked Harpe with commanding the forces on the northern side of the salient, Rendulic with those in the east and Lemelsen those in the south. Even though the Soviets had three tank armies available – the 2nd, 4th and 3rd Guards – they were not committed in a coordinated fashion. Model judiciously shifted his Panzer divisions around the shrinking salient in a classic example of interior lines, fending off one Soviet attack, then another. Soon, the Soviets found themselves in an attritional battle, but this time they got the worst of it. When Bryansk Front decided to commit the 700 tanks of General-Lieutenant Pavel S. Rybalko's 3rd Guards Tank Army on 19 July even though their infantry had failed to achieve a breakthrough against Rendulic's defences, Model calmly dispatched his remaining heavy armour to stop them. In a week of grinding tank battles, Rybalko's tank army lost 669 tanks on the approaches to Orel and had to be withdrawn from combat without achieving its objectives.

Although Model was giving all three Soviet fronts a bloody nose, his own troops were being worn down by fatigue and losses as well, so he ordered completion of the Hagen Stellung as soon as possible. He also made it a priority to evacuate 20,000 German wounded from hospitals in the Orel salient, as well as 53,000 tons of supplies. On 26 July the 500 tanks of the 4th Tank Army joined the battle, forcing the commitment of German reserves from elsewhere in Heeresgruppe Mitte. By late July the Ostheer had eight of its 16 Panzer divisions defending the Orel salient, which seriously denuded the rest of the front of armour. Model knew that he couldn't continue this battle forever and began working on Hitler using his standard formula – successful counter-attacks followed by requests for freedom of action. Hitler trusted Model and when Model promised him that he could conduct a fighting withdrawal to the Hagen Stellung that would free up Panzer units for new counter-attacks, Hitler authorized the evacuation of the Orel salient. Operation *Herbstreise* (Autumn Journey) began on 1 August, with both PzAOK 2 and AOK 9 gradually falling back towards the Hagen Stellung.

Unlike during Operation *Büffel*, the Soviets detected the German withdrawal immediately and accelerated their attacks. The XXXXVI Panzerkorps was hit particularly hard and its commander was killed. While sending his staff to establish a new headquarters in Bryansk, Model remained behind in Orel with a single staff officer. Hitler telephoned Model and demanded that he immediately blow up the main bridge over the river Oka, but Model ignored him and delayed until his rearguard, the 12. Panzer-Division, had crossed over to the west bank. On 5 August Soviet forces entered the burning and demolished city of Orel. During the next two weeks the Soviets failed to encircle Model's rearguard as it fell back from one switch line to the next. Instead, the pursuing Soviets suffered enormous losses. Operation *Kutuzov* crested on 18 August, short of the Hagen Stellung. It lasted 38 days and enabled the Soviet West, Bryansk and Central Fronts to recover the Orel salient, but at a cost of 429,890 casualties, including 112,000 dead. The three Soviet tank armies involved were badly mauled with the loss of 2,586 tanks. Altogether, PzAOK 2 and AOK 9 suffered 60,804 casualties and 250 tanks lost during the withdrawal from the Orel salient. Model had achieved another defensive victory by saving his forces from encirclement and inflicting losses of almost seven to one on his pursuers, though the enemy was far more able to replace their losses. Amazingly, Model even managed to reach the Hagen Stellung with 11,732 Soviet prisoners in tow – an unusual accomplishment for a 'defeated' army.

While Model's new defensive line around Bryansk was fairly solid, the rest of the German front line was in turmoil by August 1943. Manstein's Heeresgruppe Süd was ripped apart by the Soviet Operation *Rumyantsev* counter-offensive on 5 August and, after losing Kharkov on 23 August, was in full retreat back to the river Dnepr. Unable to budge AOK 9 and PzAOK 2, the Soviet Western Front began attacking the German AOK 4 on Model's left flank on 7 August, and then Rokossovsky's Central Front attacked AOK 2 on his right flank on 26 August. The OKH quickly stripped Model of his best infantry divisions and all but one Panzer division to reinforce his neighbours' crumbling sectors, which made his own situation problematic when the

As Operation *Kutuzov* began to squeeze the Orel salient, Model's forces kept falling back a few kilometres to the next switchback line, conducting a classic delaying operation against a superior opponent. Here a Pz IV tank and German infantry await the Soviet advance guard on the flat terrain around Orel. (Ian Barter)

Bryansk Front renewed its attacks on the Hagen Stellung on 7 September. Both AOK 2 and AOK 4 were soon in full retreat despite receiving Model's reserves and AOK 9 was now in danger of being enveloped on both flanks, so Model had little choice but to evacuate Bryansk on 17 September and fall back towards the river Dnepr. Once AOK 9 reached the new line, he gained a six-week reprieve. With his front temporarily stabilized, a weary Model applied for leave in early November, but found that Hitler had decided to place him in the Führerreserv, pending a new assignment.

Model meets with the crew of an assault gun in Heeresgruppe Nord, early February 1944. Although the situation was grim during the retreat from Leningrad, Model managed to inspire his troops to rally and stop the Soviet advance on the Panther Stellung. (Ian Barter)

Sword and Shield on the northern front, January–March 1944

Model spent the period from November 1943 to January 1944 at home in Dresden with his family. On 28 January 1944 he was suddenly ordered to report to Wolfsschanze, where Hitler informed him that he was going to relieve Generalfeldmarschall Georg Wilhelm von Küchler and that he wanted Model to take over command of Heeresgruppe Nord. The Soviet Leningrad and Volkhov Fronts had launched a massive offensive on 14 January that had shattered the German 18. Armee (AOK 18) front around Leningrad. Küchler had not only been unable to stem the Soviet onslaught, but he had ordered an unauthorized withdrawal to the Panther Stellung. Hitler was

Model keeps the river Oka bridge open for his rearguard at Orel, 4 August 1943

After the failure of Operation *Zitadelle*, Model's AOK 9 came under attack in the Orel salient by three Soviet fronts. Although Model was able to use the advantage of interior lines to shuffle his Panzer divisions around in order to prevent a Soviet breakthrough, he was forced to fight a delaying action back to the Hagen Stellung. When Soviet armour approached the burning Orel, Model remained behind in the city with a single staff officer, Major Gerd Niepold, and the rearguard 12. Panzer-Division. Fearful that the Soviets would seize the main road bridge over the Oka intact, Hitler called Model directly from East Prussia and demanded that he blow up the bridge immediately. However, Model would not abandon his rearguard on the far side of the river and he deliberately ignored Hitler's orders for most of the day. Finally, once the 12. Panzer-Division was across the Oka, the bridge was destroyed. Here, Model stands with Niepold as the 12. Panzer-Division's rearguard retreats across the bridge; a soldier on one of the vehicles waves to Model as he passes by. Meanwhile, German engineers prepare to destroy the bridge. Despite later accusations that Model was blindly obedient to Hitler, he consistently put the welfare of his troops above such concerns.

incensed by generals who would rather retreat than fight, and he ordered Model to get to Heeresgruppe Nord's headquarters in Pskov, stop the retreat, build a new front and repulse the Soviet spearheads.

Arriving in Pskov in the early hours of 31 January, Model rapidly took stock of AOK 18's situation, which was grim. On Model's northern flank, two of the Leningrad Front's armies had already reached the outskirts of Narva, which was still held by the remnants of III SS-Panzerkorps and XXVI Armeekorps. In the centre, three more Soviet armies were approaching the river Luga – which Hitler insisted must be held – but AOK 18 had barely 17,000 combat troops dispersed across a 115km-wide front. Unlike his experiences at Rzhev and Orel, Model had negligible armour or air support available in Heeresgruppe Nord, although the OKH promised that two Panzer divisions would arrive soon. Nevertheless, Model developed tactics to slow and then stop the Soviet steamroller, which he called *Schild und Schwert* (sword and shield); he would conduct tactical withdrawals in order to concentrate enough forces to conduct local counter-attacks that would recover key terrain. He also ordered the formation of hedgehog defences at Narva and Luga, as well as cannibalizing thousands of rear-area personnel to create new infantry replacements.

Model went to Narva on 2 February, where he inspected General der Infanterie Otto Sponheimer's defences. The Soviet 2nd Shock Army was preparing a major attack to capture Narva, and Sponheimer told Model that the city would fall unless it received reinforcements. Although he had little to give, Model realized that the loss of Narva would unhinge the northern half of the Panther Stellung and lead to the rapid loss of Estonia, so he rushed the Tigers of schwere Panzer Abteilung 502 to bolster the defence. He also earmarked Panzergrenadier-Division 'Feldherrnhalle' for Narva, when it arrived from Heeresgruppe Mitte. Although the Soviet 2nd Shock Army succeeded in gaining bridgeheads across the river Narva and virtually encircled the defenders, Sponheimer's troops conducted an epic and fanatical defence that repulsed all attacks for the next six months.

Once his left flank was secured, Model turned to the centre, where the remnants of XXXVIII and L Armeekorps were trying to form strongpoints around Luga. Yet even as three armies from the Volkhov Front advanced at a rate of 16km a day directly towards Luga, the Soviet 42nd Army crossed the river Luga and began enveloping the city from the west. Model ordered the first of his *Schild und Schwert* operations by directing XXVI Armeekorps to mass three divisions and then

A platoon of German StuG III assault guns move up for a counter-attack near Narva, early February 1944. Although most of Model's *Schild und Schwert* counter-attacks failed to stop the Soviet advance, Gruppe Sponheimer performed a defensive miracle at Narva that stopped any further Soviet gains in this critical sector for the next six months. (Ian Barter)

counter-attack the 42nd Army to stop its envelopment. Even with the weak 12. Panzer-Division added to the attack, it was not an imposing strike force. The attack on 9–10 February ended up becoming a confused meeting engagement that only briefly slowed the Soviet advance and decimated the units involved. When the Soviets managed to encircle and destroy one German infantry regiment, even Hitler became concerned that AOK 18 was about to be surrounded, and he authorized the evacuation of the Luga position. Despite Model's tough talk about holding on and counter-attacking, for once Hitler gave in to reason and ordered Heeresgruppe Nord to fall back to the Panther Stellung. By 1 March Heeresgruppe Nord's front had stabilized for the time, and a grateful Hitler promoted Model to *Generalfeldmarschall*. At 53, Model was the youngest *Generalfeldmarschall* in the Wehrmacht.

Model talks to a German machine-gun crew in Heeresgruppe Nord, March 1944. Model always maintained an ability to talk to front-line soldiers and he used constant interaction with his troops to monitor their morale and fighting capabilities. (Author)

The Führer's fireman, March–August 1944

The crisis on Heeresgruppe Nord's front had barely abated when a new emergency arose in western Ukraine. Manstein's Heeresgruppe Süd had been pursued across Ukraine since its defeat at Kursk and had been unable to form an effective front in the face of relentless attacks. An offensive by Zhukov's 1st Ukrainian Front and Konev's 2nd Ukrainian Front managed to encircle the 1. Panzerarmee (PzAOK 1), commanded by Model's old classmate Generaloberst Hans-Valentin Hube, around Kamenets-Podolsky on 28 March. Hube's Pocket – which contained 20 divisions with over 200,000 troops – was the largest encirclement of German forces on the Eastern Front since Stalingrad. Unfortunately, seven of the nine Panzer divisions assigned to Heeresgruppe Süd were inside the pocket, and its remaining formations – Generaloberst Erhard Raus' PzAOK 4 and the Hungarian First Army – were too weak to rescue Hube. Two days later, Hitler relieved Manstein of command and ordered Model to take over the redesignated Heeresgruppe Nordukraine.

When Model arrived at his new headquarters in Proskurov he continued with the rescue plan developed by Manstein, which was to have Hube's encircled army push westwards to link up with a rescue force. Hitler consented to transferring II SS-Panzerkorps from Belgium to provide the nucleus of an armoured rescue force, and this plan unfolded in Model's first week in command. Because of Zhukov's overconfidence about annihilating the trapped Germans he was slow to notice that Hube was fighting his way westwards or that SS reinforcements were en route. On 7 April Hube linked up with II SS-Panzerkorps and his army was reintegrated back into a cohesive front. Model deployed PzAOK 1 and PzAOK 4 in an arc around the city of L'vov in southern Poland, which is where both he and Hitler expected the

Soviets to make their next big push. He left the Hungarian First Army to cover the Carpathian mountain passes and to maintain a tenuous link with Heeresgruppe Südukraine.

Although PzAOK 1 was saved, it had lost most of its tanks and artillery in escaping the pocket. Model had 475,000 troops under his command but the divisions were now threadbare, with limited firepower and mobility. A particularly distressing incident for morale was the Soviet encirclement of the 4,500-man Gruppe Neinhoff in Tarnopol, which Hitler had designated as a *Festung* (places designated *Festung* were to be defended to the last man). Model mounted a desperate rescue effort from 11–20 April with over 100 tanks, but the Panzers were stopped by mud and Soviet resistance 8km short of a link-up with the trapped garrison; only 55 survivors reached German lines. Generalmajor Egon von Neinhoff and the rest of his troops were annihilated when the pocket was overrun. After this the Germans gained a brief respite in May since the muddy season inhibited operations, but Model pressed the OKH for reinforcements to help defeat the expected Soviet summer advance upon L'vov. Unfortunately, the OKH decided to transfer several divisions from Heeresgruppe Mitte to reinforce Model but failed to detect the buildup of Soviet forces in Byelorussia.

In mid-June 1944, Heeresgruppe Mitte was commanded by Model's old superior from AOK 16 in France, Generalfeldmarschall Ernst Busch. From north to south, his command comprised PzAOK 3, AOK 4, AOK 9 and AOK 2, with 36 divisions and 580,000 men. However, Busch's infantry units were well understrength and he had only a single Panzer division in reserve. Busch knew that a Soviet offensive against his front was imminent, so he formed a strong defensive line based on the fortified cities of Vitebsk, Orsha, Mogilev and Bobruisk and concentrated his armour and best units in the centre with AOK 4. He also assumed that he could hold this line long enough for reinforcements to arrive from neighbouring army groups. Unfortunately, this was no longer 1942 and Zhukov had learned his lesson about taking apart a prepared German defence. When Operation *Bagration* began on 22 June, four Soviet fronts began a series of sequenced attacks that rapidly demolished Heeresgruppe Mitte's entire front. Instead of striking the strong German centre, Zhukov began by attacking the more vulnerable flanks; while he attacked and encircled part of PzAOK 3 at Vitebsk, Rokossovsky did the same thing to AOK 9 at Bobruisk. Within six days, Heeresgruppe Mitte's flanks had been smashed in, all four fortified cities were lost or encircled and AOK 4 was in full retreat back to Minsk. When Busch proved helpless to stop the Soviet avalanche, Hitler relieved him on 28 June and turned to his trusted 'fireman', Walther Model, to extinguish the blaze.

Model in his Sd. Kfz. 251 command half-track during the Tarnopol rescue operation in mid-April 1944. Model became personally involved in trying to rescue the trapped 4,500-man garrison of Gruppe Neinhoff, but despite his best efforts only 55 survivors reached German lines. (Nik Cornish, WH 743)

While retaining command of Heeresgruppe Nordukraine, Model was given operational control over Heeresgruppe Mitte (he left Josef Harpe as acting commander at L'vov). When Model arrived in Minsk the situation facing him was catastrophic. Heeresgruppe Mitte had already suffered 190,000 casualties – a third of its strength – and only AOK 4 in the centre and AOK 2 on the distant right flank had any combat power left. It must have been disheartening even for a tough soldier like Model to find his former commands, XXXXI Panzerkorps and AOK 9, surrounded in the Bobruisk Pocket and on the verge of annihilation. Everywhere the Soviets were advancing at a gallop, with the most threatening being the 5th Guards Tank Army bridgehead across the river Berezina at Borisov. For any other commander, this would have been a hopeless and soul-crushing experience, but Model was at his best in a desperate crisis. Hitler ordered Model to hold Minsk, but even before he could begin to arrange a defence, the Soviet 5th Guards Tank Army broke out of its bridgehead and encircled the bulk of the retreating AOK 4 east of Minsk. Model shifted remnants of AOK 9 to build a hedgehog defence around Minsk, and he moved the full-strength 5. Panzer-Division from Heeresgruppe Nordukraine in order to try and open an escape route for the trapped AOK 4 and keep the 5th Guards Tank Army at bay. Some troops managed to escape the pocket, but the bulk of AOK 4 was destroyed and the 5. Panzer-Division lost 86 per cent of its armour in a week's heavy fighting. On 3 July the 5th Guards Tank Army entered Minsk. In less than two weeks Heeresgruppe Mitte had lost 26 divisions and 300,000 men, leaving Model with no choice but to cede Byelorussia and fall back to the Polish border.

After the capture of Minsk, the Soviet armies continued to advance westwards, reaching the Polish border by mid-July. Model began repairing Heeresgruppe Mitte's line by first rebuilding its flanks, using the relatively intact AOK 2 to build a line anchored on Brest-Litovsk, while PzAOK 4 sidestepped northwards to become his right flank. The OKH transferred several divisions from Ukraine and Estonia to help protect East Prussia, but the reinforcements drawn from the flanking army groups proved to be problematic when the Stavka unleashed major offensives on these fronts as well. By mid-July the Soviet 2nd Baltic Front was pushing back AOK 16 on Heeresgruppe Nord's right flank and the 1st Ukrainian Front had begun the L'vov–Sandomierz offensive against Heeresgruppe Nordukraine. Although Harpe mounted a tough defence, the 1st Ukrainian Front overwhelmed it and captured L'vov on 27 July, then pushed on towards the Vistula.

In central Poland Model had rebuilt a very thin continuous front by 17 July, but Rokossovsky's 1st Byelorussian Front still had plenty of fight left in it. Rokossovsky massed three armies against PzAOK 4's positions near Kovel and blasted an 80km-wide hole in their line, then pushed the 2nd Tank Army through with orders to advance northwest towards Warsaw. Simultaneously, Rokossovsky began enveloping AOK 2's positions at Brest, threatening to encircle eight more divisions. By 23 July Heeresgruppe Mitte's front was broken once again, with a 95km-wide gap between PzAOK 4 and AOK 2. With nothing left in their way, the Soviet 2nd Tank Army marched 120km through

Generalfeldmarschall Model instructs troops on the proper sighting of their MG 42 machine gun, North Ukraine, May 1944. As the quality of German replacements declined Model made greater efforts to ensure that they were properly trained – something that Allied commanders failed to do. (Author)

the flat Polish countryside in three days and gained a bridgehead across the Vistula at Magnuszew. On top of these new disasters, news came of the attempted assassination of Adolf Hitler on 20 July. Model was the first Generalfeldmarschall to transmit a message to the Wolfsschanze reaffirming his loyalty to the Führer – which earned him points with Hitler.

By 28 July Rokossovsky's 2nd Tank Army was on the outskirts of Warsaw and Brest had fallen, but the Soviet offensive was running out of steam. Having advanced 565km in the past five weeks, the Soviet spearheads had outrun their supplies and air support. Furthermore, the four fronts involved in Operation *Bagration* had suffered 765,000 casualties in this period and lost 4,000 tanks. In contrast, the German supply situation improved as they fell back towards Warsaw, and by late July the OKH was directing a steady stream of reinforcements to Model, including IV SS-Panzerkorps ('Wiking' and 'Totenkopf' Panzer divisions), the Fallschirm-Panzer-Division 'Hermann Göring' from Italy and the 19. Panzer-Division from Holland. Model massed these Panzer units for a major counter-attack against the 2nd Tank Army outside Warsaw from 31 July to 5 August. Although one Soviet tank corps was badly mangled and the 2nd Tank Army was pushed back 19km, the German counter-attack failed to inflict a decisive defeat on Rokossovsky's front.

Despite the apparently hopeless situation on the Eastern Front, the Armia Krajowa (Polish Home Army) and Stalin came to Model's rescue. When the Armia Krajowa rose in revolt against the German garrison in Warsaw on 1 August and seized part of the city, Stalin made the political decision to suspend offensive operations in central Poland so that the Germans could eliminate the Polish resistance. Despite the fact that Model's troops were on the ropes, Stalin pulled the 2nd Tank Army back from Warsaw to refit, and the rest of Rokossovsky's front contented itself with slowly pushing AOK 2 back to the river Narew. Model was astounded by Rokossovsky's switch in tactics, but seized upon the lull in operations to rebuild Heeresgruppe Mitte. Leaving the reduction of the Armia Krajowa in Warsaw to the SS, Model transferred two Panzer divisions to counter-attack the Magnuszew bridgehead and used IV SS-Panzerkorps to stitch up holes in his line north of Warsaw. The OKH sent Model 12 of the Wave 29 Volksgrenadier Divisions, which he used to rebuild his shattered armies. Amazingly, by mid-August Model had built a new, stronger line along the Vistula–Narew front, which would hold for the next five months. Model had not done anything brilliant; his main accomplishments were not losing his head, displaying a ruthless willingness to sacrifice blocking units to buy time and demonstrating the agility needed to seize fleeting opportunities.

The 'Miracle in the West', August–November 1944

> We have lost a battle, but I tell you, we shall still win this war… This hour
> will separate the real men from the weaklings.
> *Model, 3 September 1944*

For his accomplishment in restoring the front in central Poland, Model was
called to Hitler's Wolfsschanze headquarters on 15 August 1944, where
he was awarded the Third Reich's highest award – the Knight's Cross with
Oak Leaves, Swords and Diamonds. Afterwards, Hitler told him that he had
a new assignment for his miracle-worker. Within two months of the Allied
landing in Normandy the German forces in France were being bled to death,
and a collapse of the front was imminent. Hitler had lost confidence in
Generalfeldmarschall Günther von Kluge, the current *Oberbefehlshaber West*
(commander-in-chief west), whose defeatist attitude was as evident as his
inability to stop the Allied advance. In his place, Hitler appointed Model as
both *Oberbefehlshaber West* and commander of Heeresgruppe B, and ordered
him to 'build up a new western front as far forward of the Seine–Yvonne
line as possible'. Although Hitler had no reinforcements to give Model,
he proved unusually reasonable by authorizing Heeresgruppe G to withdraw
from southern France.

Youthful Volksgrenadier
soldiers head to the
Western Front in
September 1944. A large
part of Model's 'Miracle
in the West' was the Third
Reich's ability to raise
formations of untrained
recruits and rush them
to garrison Aachen and
the Westwall before the
sluggish Allied vanguards
arrived. (Ian Barter)

When Model arrived at *Oberbefehlshaber West* headquarters in Château de
La Roche Guyon on the evening of 17 August, he found that – as usual – the
situation was desperate and rapidly becoming catastrophic. Both AOK 7 and
5. Panzerarmee (PzAOK 5) were nearly surrounded inside the Falaise Pocket
by the Canadian First Army while Patton's Third US Army was running
almost unopposed up the Loire Valley. In southern France, Allied landings
made Heeresgruppe G's situation equally critical. Although Model issued
a typically impulsive order to subordinate units to hold at all costs – primarily
to display his 'iron resolve' to Hitler – he immediately began trying to salvage
Heeresgruppe B by ordering it to withdraw to the river Seine, and ordered

Heeresgruppe G to fall back to
Dijon. Equally typical, he jumped
into his staff car the next morning
and went to the front, setting up
a tactical headquarters at Fontaine
l'Abbe outside the Falaise Pocket.
Model's priority was to save
the best armour units, such as
II SS-Panzerkorps, which he used
to mount a counter-attack against
the Polish 1st Armoured Division
blocking the only remaining exit
route from the Falaise Pocket.
Although the Allies closed the
Falaise Pocket on 21 August,

Model was able to help evacuate at least 40,000 veteran troops.

Hard on their heels, Allied troops advanced on Paris, and when the US 79th Infantry Division began crossing the Seine, Model had to evacuate his headquarters at La Roche Guyon. Model was unwilling to commit his limited remaining forces to defend Paris but he deliberately used his *Schild und Schwert* tactics to slow down the Allied advance. Nevertheless, Allied forces still poured into Paris and the German garrison

Generalfeldmarschal Model visits the forward command bunker of the 246. Volksgrenadier-Division on 9 October 1944. This hastily formed unit had just entered the battle for Aachen and was forced to surrender two weeks later, but it bought valuable time for Model to rebuild Heeresgruppe B's front line. (Bundesarchiv, Bild 183-1992-0617-506, Fotograf: Scheerer)

there surrendered on 25 August. The remnants of the shattered Heeresgruppe B fell back in disorder towards Belgium and the German border.

Unlike in Poland, Model had no armoured reinforcements on the way and his only intact force was General der Infanterie Gustav von Zangen's weak 15. Armee (AOK 15), comprised of six low-quality infantry divisions deployed on the Channel coast. Initially, Model hoped that Zangen's divisions could build a new line on the river Somme, but Model's opponents had huge advantages in mobility, intelligence and air superiority, which allowed them to act more quickly than the Wehrmacht. Using information gleaned from ULTRA intercepts, Lieutenant-General Omar Bradley redirected the First US Army to conduct a pincer operation that killed or captured another 28,500 of Model's troops inside the Mons Pocket. Falling back to a new headquarters near Liege, Model's situational awareness deteriorated rapidly; his communications with his surviving forces were so disrupted that he had little idea where they or the enemy were located.

1   20–21 August: Model orders II SS-Panzerkorps to attack in order to reopen an escape corridor for the trapped AOK 7 and PzAOK 5 in the Falaise Pocket.

2   21 August: Model orders a counter-attack against the Third US Army bridgehead over the Seine.

3   25 August: After Model decides not to commit forces to hold Paris; the German garrison in the city surrenders.

4   26–30 August: Model tries to form a delaying position on the river Somme with AOK 15 but the Allies overrun this area before German forces can establish a defence.

5   28–30 August: Model masses his remaining armour – about 100 tanks – near Rheims to block Third US Army's direct advance towards the Saar.

6   31 August: First US Army encircles 70,000 German survivors from AOK 7 in the Mons Pocket.

7   2 September: Eisenhower temporarily halts First and Third US Armies because of fuel shortages.

8   3–4 September: The British Second Army captures Brussels and Antwerp. Model scrambles to assemble blocking forces in order to stop any further advance.

9   5 September: Runstedt arrives in Koblenz to resume his duties as OB West.

10   5 September: AOK 15 begins crossing the Scheldt estuary; some forces are sent to hold the Albert Canal while others remain to hold the estuary.

11   5–10 September: The newly formed 1. Fallschirm-Armee begins creating a new front line in Holland. The British advance slows to a crawl.

12   6–12 September: Model sends his few reinforcements to concentrate around Aachen and Trier.

13   13 September: The battle of the Breskens Pocket begins, with AOK 15 putting up heavy resistance against Canadian First Army.

14   15 September: The First and Ninth US Armies reach the Westwall near Aachen and begin a limited offensive.

15   17 September: Operation *Market Garden* begins in Holland, but the Germans score a defensive victory at Arnhem by 26 September.

16   19 September: The First US Army begins its advance into the Hürtgen Forest.

Model's Operations in the West, 18 August to 26 September 1944

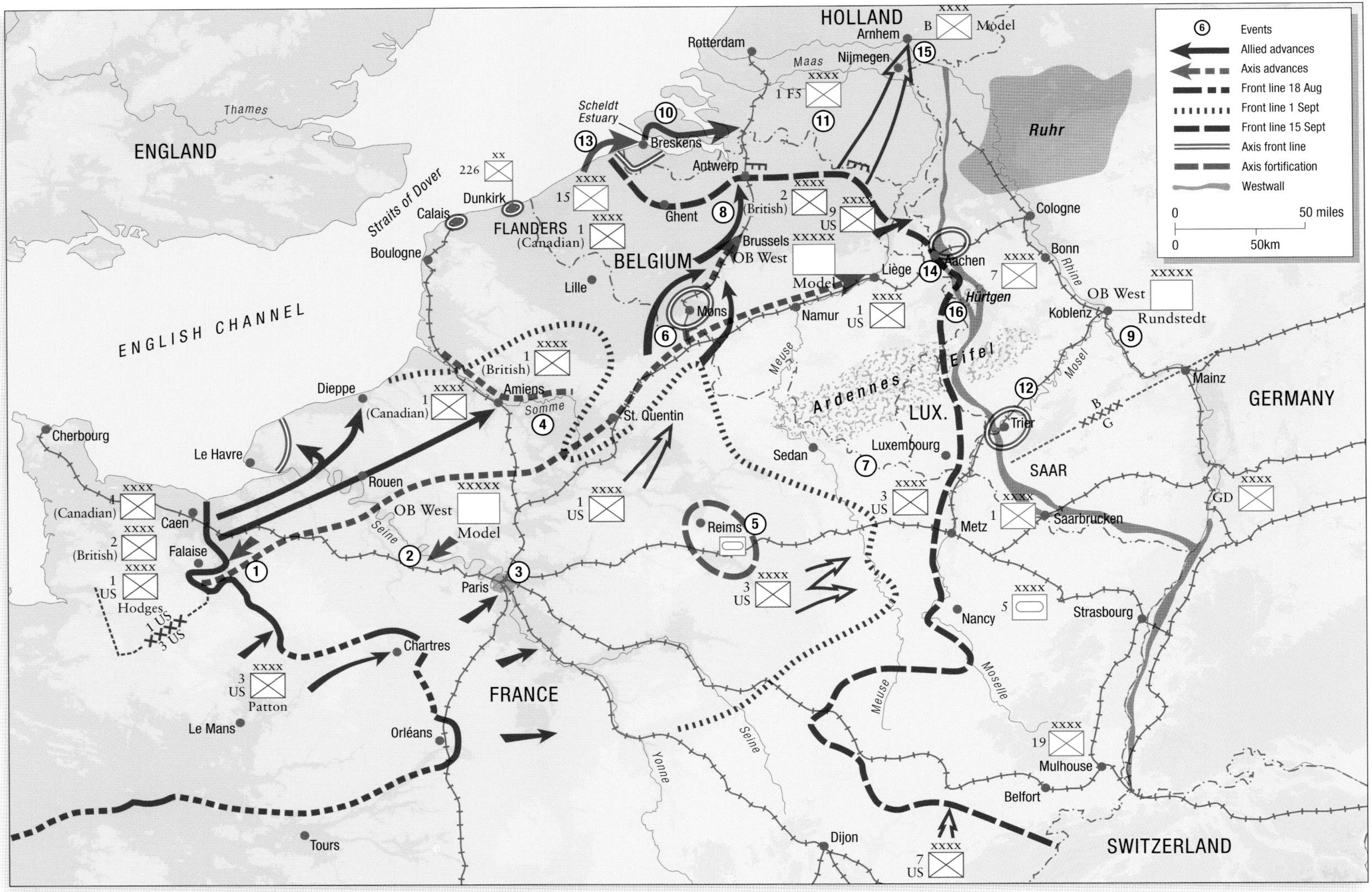

Legend:

Events

Allied advances

Axis advances

Front line 18 Aug

Front line 1 Sept

Front line 15 Sept

Axis front line

Axis fortification

Westwall

0   50km
0   50 miles

Labels:

ENGLAND

Thames

Strait of Dover

ENGLISH CHANNEL

GERMANY

SWITZERLAND

HOLLAND

Amsterdam / Arnhem

Nijmegen

Rotterdam

Maas

BELGIUM

Antwerp

Ghent

Brussels

Breskens

Scheldt Estuary

FLANDERS

Lille

Dunkirk

Calais

Boulogne

Dieppe

Le Havre

Rouen

Amiens

Somme

St. Quentin

Paris

Seine

Chartres

Orléans

Tours

Le Mans

Caen

Falaise

Cherbourg

Reims

Sedan

Namur

Liège

Aachen

Hürtgen

Eifel

Ardennes

LUX.

Luxembourg

Meuse

Meuse

Yonne

Dijon

SAAR

Metz

Nancy

Moselle

Strasbourg

Saarbrücken

Mulhouse

Belfort

Mainz

Koblenz

Mosel

Trier

Bonn

Cologne

Rhine

Ruhr

OB West

Rundstedt

Model

Hodges

Patton

Aptwerp

The real crisis came in the first week of September 1944. Before Zangen's static divisions could be shifted to create a new line on the Albert Canal, the British XXX Corps advanced into a virtually undefended Belgium and liberated Brussels on 3 September. The next day the British 11th Armoured Division made a 105km dash to capture the vital port of Antwerp, which also nearly isolated Zangen's army on the coast. At that point, only the solitary 719. Infanterie-Division and a Dutch SS brigade stood between the British XXX Corps and the approaches to the Ruhr. However, just as his command faced utter catastrophe, Model's luck held thanks to a combination of enemy mistakes and energetic subordinates. Instead of seizing two nearby bridges across the Albert Canal, the British 11th Armoured Division paused in Antwerp. The commander of the 719. Infanterie-Division seized the moment, destroying both bridges and forming a thin defence along the canal. Generalleutnant Kurt Chill also managed to form another *Kampfgruppe* of survivors on the eastern end of the canal. When the British finally resumed their advance two days later, the German defences on the canal held.

Model conferring with a junior officer during the desperate defence of Aachen. Model's repuation for restoring order from catastrophic defeats helped to restore morale on the shattered Western Front and enabled the remnants of Heeresgruppe B to temporarily halt the Allied advance on the Westwall. (Author)

The sudden loss of Brussels and Antwerp caused a brief panic in the Wehrmacht, extending from units running for their lives all the way up the high command. Even Model's confidence suffered a jolt from this news and he informed the OKW that he had almost no forces left with which to build a new front and needed at least 30 fresh divisions. Yet the OKW had no fresh divisions to send. In a situation conference at Wolfsschanze, Göring told Hitler that he would release six regiments of *Fallschirmjäger* trainees and 10,000 unemployed Luftwaffe ground personnel to Model, which would form the 1. Fallschirm-Armee and would defend Holland. Generaloberst Kurt Student, one of Hitler's favourite Luftwaffe generals, would command the new formation.

Despite these impressive-sounding promises, Model knew that he would still have very few troops with which to defend either Holland or the German border for at least another month. The British finally got a bridgehead across the Albert Canal on 8 September and Student's flimsy command could not hold for long. However, Model took full advantage of the British failure to exploit their success at Antwerp by evacuating 86,000 troops from the isolated AOK 15 across the Scheldt Estuary; these troops were used to reinforce Student's defences and brought the British advance into Holland to a halt. Montgomery's failure to seize the Beveland Isthmus near Antwerp and thereby prevent the escape of AOK 15 was a huge mistake that aided the German recovery. As usual, Model put a premium on front-line intelligence and his Ic deduced that the British would soon mount a major push into Holland to outflank the Ruhr, likely employing airborne landings.

To the amazement of the Germans, Montgomery halted the bulk of his forces for over a week in order to rest, refuel and refit. On 11 September Model moved his headquarters to the Tafelberg Hotel in Oosterbeek, near Arnhem. Although the vanguard of the First US Army reached the German border near Aachen on the same day, Model assessed Montgomery as the most immediate threat and moved his headquarters to a place where he could control the battle for Holland. He also made the decision to relocate II SS-Panzerkorps to the Arnhem area, where it could provide him with a limited mobile reserve while it was rebuilding. Either by intuition

A Tiger tank from schwere Panzer Abteilung 506 near Geilenkirchen on 15 October 1944. Model used the Tigers to reinforce a counter-attack against the American 1st Infantry Division in an effort to prevent two American corps from encircling Aachen. Despite inflicting some losses, the counter-attack failed and US forces completed the encirclement of Aachen the next day. (Ian Barter)

or luck, Model had made decisions that would prevent the Allies from ending the war in 1944. Hitler eased Model's burden slightly by reappointing Generalfeldmarschall Gerd von Rundstedt as *OB West*, leaving Model to worry about Heeresgruppe B only, while Generaloberst Johannes Blaskowitz's Heeresgruppe G guarded Alsace-Lorraine.

While a major battle was shaping up for Holland, Model also had to keep an eye on the German border between Aachen and the Hürtgen Forest, where Hodges' First US Army was already engaged by 13 September. The Westwall was only held by remnants of AOK 7 and Model was forced to commit his very limited armour and infantry reserves to prevent Aachen from being encircled. Increased German resistance, combined with supply difficulties and rainy weather, caused the over-cautious Hodges to call off the offensive just as Model's line was about to break. Model used the lull to reinforce this sector with Volksgrenadier units and to emplace extensive minefields.

On 17 September Montgomery made his move into Holland with Operation *Market Garden*, dropping three airborne divisions along the Eindhoven–Nijmegen–Arnhem corridor in order to seize bridges that would allow XXX Corps' tanks to outflank the Westwall defences. Model himself was taken aback when the British 1st Airborne Division began landing within 5km of his headquarters at the Tafelberg Hotel, and he had to evacuate post haste. For a moment it seemed that Montgomery would demolish Model's flimsy defences and score a major breakthrough. Once again however, Model's luck held because of the arrogant oversight of his opponents; not only had Allied intelligence missed the relocation of II SS-Panzerkorps to Arnhem – which doomed the British landing – but a copy of the Allied plan was captured on the first day, which revealed to Model that destroying the Nijmegen Bridge would derail Montgomery's entire plan. Furthermore, XXX Corps' efforts to push up the main road from Eindhoven took so long that Model was able to crush the British at Arnhem while building a strong defence at Nijmegen. Then Model made a rare tactical mistake by deciding not to blow up the Nijmegen Bridge because he wanted it intact for a possible German counter-attack. Instead,

the British and Americans succeeded in suddenly capturing the bridge, but were still unable to link up with the trapped British paratroopers at Arnhem. Montgomery was forced to evacuate his bridgehead across the Lower Rhine and his plans for a rapid envelopment of the Ruhr had turned to ashes. Model had achieved another defensive victory, defeating Montgomery and inflicting over 13,000 casualties on the Allies.

Some 5,600 British paratroopers surrendered at Arnhem in September 1944. The destruction of the British 1st Airborne Division paralyzed Montgomery's 21st Army Group for the next five months and gave Model a respite to rebuild the German defences in Holland. (Bundesarchiv 101I-497-3529-10, Fotograf: Jacobsen)

Yet just as Model had stopped Montgomery in his tracks he had to turn back to deal with Hodges' renewed offensives against Aachen and the Hürtgen Forest. Model fought a desperate three-week battle with his hotchpotch units to prevent the US VII and XIX Corps from closing the pincers around Aachen, and was able to seriously delay the American timetable. Ultimately, Hodges' forces were able to encircle Aachen and the city fell on 21 October. However, Model won a consolation victory in the two-month-long battle for the Hürtgen Forest, where he skilfully used his limited infantry, artillery and engineers to decimate four American divisions, which were committed piecemeal. After suffering 24,000 casualties, Hodges had still not cleared the forest. When Hodges launched a multi-corps offensive on 16 November to reach the dams on the river Roer, Model conducted a stubborn defence, delaying the Americans for another three weeks. By early December Hodges' offensive had been stopped short of the dams. All told, Model's dogged defence of the Westwall had inflicted 57,000 casualties on the First and Ninth

Model confers with the commanders of II SS-Panzerkorps in response to the British airborne landing at Arnhem, 1500hrs, 17 September 1944

After fleeing from the British airborne landings near his headquarters at the Tafelberg hotel in Oosterbeek, Model went to SS-Obergruppenführer Wilhelm Bittrich's headquarters east of Arnhem at Doetinchem, where he took personal control of the battle. A copy of the *Market Garden* plan had already been captured from an Allied glider, which provided Model with an unparalleled insight into the enemy objectives. Seizing this opportunity, Model quickly began issuing orders to Bittrich's II SS-Panzerkorps that would doom *Market Garden* to failure. He ordered SS-Gruppenführer Heinz Harmel, commander of the 10. SS-Panzer-Division 'Frundsberg', to secure Nijmegen Bridge against the American 82nd Airborne Division, while SS-Obersturmbannführer Walther Harzer's 9. SS-Panzer-Division 'Hohenstaufen' crushed the British landings at Arnhem. This scene shows Model just after he arrived, conferring with Bittrich, Harmel and Harzer and making the key tactical decisions, while German troops march by in the background, heading towards Arnhem. Model and Bittrich were able to assemble mixed *Kampfgruppen* from nearby Waffen SS, Army and Luftwaffe troops and dispatch them towards the British airborne landings at Arnhem.

During the battle for Arnhem, Model meets with SS-Brigadeführer Heinz Harmel, commander of the 10. SS-Panzer-Division 'Frundsberg'. Model assigned Harmel the mission of preventing the American 82nd Airborne Division from seizing the vital Nijmegen Bridge. Harmel wanted to destroy the bridge immediately but Model refused, since he wanted to use it for a possible counter-attack later. This proved to be one of Model's few tactical mistakes. (Bundesarchiv, Bild 183-J27784, Fotograf: Peter Adendorf)

US Armies and destroyed 650 tanks, although German losses were also heavy. After three months of never-ending crises, Model finally succeeded in stabilizing Heeresgruppe B's front. Taken together, the battles of Arnhem and the Hürtgen Forest were impressive defensive victories that robbed the Allies of the initiative and helped to restore German front-line morale.

Wacht am Rhein, December 1944 to January 1945

We lack hard men like Model, Dietrich and Rudel.
Hitler, 28 December 1944

In December 1944 Hitler decided to reorganize the command structure on the Western Front. Model retained command of Heeresgruppe B with 7. Armee (AOK 7), AOK 15 and PzAOK 5, but became responsible only for the northwest German border. A new Heeresgruppe H was created to defend Holland, while Heeresgruppe G continued to guard the southern German border down to Switzerland.

Model and Runstedt were first made aware on 22 October of plans for a counter-offensive designated *Wacht am Rhein*. They also learned that they would have to fight the autumn defensive battles with the absolute minimum of forces, while the OKW sent 16,000 replacements to rebuild divisions for the upcoming offensive. Given the poor state of the Wehrmacht in late 1944, neither Model nor Rundstedt were sanguine about the prospects for mounting a successful large-scale counter-offensive. Furthermore, half the fuel that the OKH reserved for *Wacht am Rhein* was consumed in the fighting along the Westwall in October–November 1944; Model and Rundstedt knew that there simply wasn't enough left to reach grand objectives like Antwerp. Instead, both preferred to employ Germany's remaining armoured reserves in local counter-attacks to keep the Allies off balance. Model developed a counter-offensive plan known as Operation *Herbstnebel* (Autumn Mist), which proposed an attack through the Ardennes to disrupt the First US Army and then a pivot northwards to encircle American forces around Aachen. Both Rundstedt and Model desired this kind of 'small solution' that limited operations to remain east of the Meuse and focus on destroying some of the more exposed US infantry divisions. However, Hitler realized that limited counter-attacks would only delay the inevitable Allied victory and, trusting to his 'gambler's luck', he believed that Model might pull off a miracle.

Although Model had nothing to do with the development of *Wacht am Rhein*, he was made the operational commander for the counter-offensive, which intended to smash the unwary VIII Corps of Hodges' First Army in the Ardennes Forest and then drive on to recapture the vital port of Antwerp. Both

Bradley and Hodges had decided to turn the Ardennes sector into a 'rest area' for divisions exhausted by fighting in the Hürtgen Forest, but the four divisions in VIII Corps were forced to hold a 145km-wide front and without significant tactical reserves. Even worse, Bradley and Hodges disregarded indications from VIII Corps of a possible German counter-offensive in the Ardennes, which ensured that First Army was unprepared to deal with such a contingency. In order to demolish VIII Corps, Model was given the newly formed 6. Panzerarmee (PzAOK 6) under SS-Oberstgruppenführer Josef Dietrich, with four rebuilt SS-Panzer divisions, to spearhead the offensive. Model's two other armies, General der Panzertruppen Hasso von Manteuffel's PzAOK 5 and AOK 7, also received enough replacements to enable them to participate in the counter-offensive. All told, Heeresgruppe B committed 27 divisions, including eight Panzer divisions, to attack seven American divisions.

The offensive opened on 16 December and caught First US Army totally by surprise. Despite worrying delays and unexpectedly heavy resistance on the northern flank, the Panzer divisions achieved some success in the early days of the offensive by inflicting heavy losses on several American divisions and encircling 12,000 US troops at Bastogne. As usual, Model did not remain in his headquarters but visited his troops to gauge the front-line situation. When PzAOK 6 became ensnarled in a massive traffic jam along the choked roads outside St Vith, Model directed traffic personally in order to resolve the congestion. In contrast, Bradley spent that evening in Paris playing bridge with Eisenhower and Hodges failed to react. Nevertheless, *Wacht am Rhein*'s spark faded rapidly as Allied reinforcements poured into the Ardennes and the German spearheads ran out of fuel short of the Meuse. Realizing that he could not reach the Meuse, Model continued to order attacks against Bastogne as late as 3 January 1945 in the hope of achieving one last tactical victory, but his forces could not take the town. At this point, realizing that an Allied counter-offensive to snip off the German salient was inevitable, Model urged Hitler to authorize Heeresgruppe B to withdraw to the Westwall, but the Führer was unwilling to voluntarily surrender any more territory. After a brief lull, the First and Third US Armies began attacking the flanks of the German 'bulge' in early January 1945, and by the end of the month Model's troops were back at their starting positions. German losses in the Ardennes were crippling, with over 80,000 casualties and half their tanks lost, neither of which could be replaced. Even worse, German morale now began to deteriorate and there was little that valiant speeches or fanatical commanders could do to disguise the fact that Germany had lost the war.

Model meets with Generalfeldmarshall Runstedt (OB West) at Bad Tönisstein near Koblenz in November 1944 to discuss the planning for Operation *Wacht Am Rhein*. Neither commander was optimistic about success. General der Infanterie Hans Krebs, chief of staff of Heeresgruppe B, is on the right. (Author)

The last measure, February–April 1945

German infantry advance in the Ardennes during Operation *Wacht am Rhein* in December 1944. Although these troops are armed with the superb Sturmgewehr 44 assault rifle, the quality of training of the new Volksgrenadier units was poor compared to German infantry divisions of 1943. (Bundesarchiv, Bild 183-1985-0104-501)

After the defeat in the Ardennes, the next several months had a tragic inevitability for Germany. Hitler would not allow Model to withdraw his defeated forces from the Westwall and retreat behind the Rhine, which exposed them to the inevitable Allied offensives that began in February 1945. However, Hitler stripped Heeresgruppe B of PzAOK 6 and sent it to Hungary, which fatally compromised any hope for Model of repeating the defensive successes of autumn 1944. Furthermore, the OKH announced on 1 March that there would be no more replacements for Heeresgruppe B, which reduced Model's options to little more than static defence. With most of the last reserves of fuel and ammunition expended in the Ardennes, Model's remaining Panzer units had limited mobility, and his artillery – heretofore the bedrock of his defensive tactics – was reduced to firing only four rounds per battery each day. Taking advantage of Heeresgruppe B's weakness, the Canadian First Army cleared the 1. Fallschirmarmee out of the Reichswald, then the Ninth US Army launched Operation *Grenade* against Model's exposed AOK 15 on 23 February. By 3 March the Canadians and Americans had joined, trapping 52,000 German troops on the west side of the Rhine.

The US First and Third Armies struck the rest of Model's front with Operation *Lumberjack* on 2 March, which quickly eliminated any remaining German forces west of the Rhine. Although Hitler forbade Model from pulling any of his threatened divisions back across the river, Model ignored him and succeeded in saving a few units. Yet when the American 9th Infantry Division captured the Ordensburg Vogelsang, a special Nazi Party training centre in the Eifel, Hitler became enraged and demanded that the commander of LXXIV Armeekorps and several of his subordinates be court martialled for the loss of this facility. An army-level trial quickly acquitted the officers, but Hitler demanded that Model, as the senior responsible officer, should reopen the proceedings. After carefully reviewing the facts, Model acquitted the accused officers. When Hitler tried to refer the officers to a special tribunal – which would likely have ended in a firing squad – Model used his authority to block this effort. Once again, Model had demonstrated both his willingness to stand up to the Führer and his loyalty towards his subordinates. Shortly afterwards, Model was shocked to learn about the British fire-bombing of his home city of Dresden on the night of 13–14 February. For several days, Model was uncertain of the fate of his wife and daughter in the firestorm that killed 22,000 people in the city. When called to Berlin for a conference with the

Führer two days later, Model requested permission to visit the city to look for his family, but Hitler refused. Instead, Model sent his adjutant, Oberst Pilling, who found Model's wife and daughter and evacuated them to Model's brother's house in Mühlhausen.

Distracted by military tribunals and the Dresden bombing, Model made one of his rare tactical mistakes as the First US Army raced towards the Rhine, but it was a costly one. Convinced that Hodges' forces were heading towards Bonn, Model directed his retreating units to concentrate there, ignoring the possibility that the Americans might head for the bridge at Remagen instead. Amazingly, the US 9th Armoured Division captured the bridge at Remagen intact on 7 March, which dashed any hope that the Rhine would provide a bulwark against the Allied offensives. Model tried to seal off the American bridgehead, but his Panzer units were too depleted and short of fuel to mount a successful counter-attack. Instead, he ordered AOK 15 to create defences along the river Sieg facing south in order to prevent the Americans from striking north directly into the Ruhr. Because of the disaster at Remagen, Hitler relieved Rundstedt again and replaced him as *OB West* with Generalfeldmarschall Albert Kesselring.

On 24 March 1945 Montgomery's 21st Army Group began crossing the Rhine on Heeresgruppe B's right flank and the Ninth US Army began driving a wedge between Heeresgruppe B and Heeresgruppe H in Holland. Model ordered PzAOK 5 to build a defence along the river Lippe and Dortmund–Ems Canal against the Ninth US Army. The next day, the First US Army broke out of the Remagen bridgehead on Model's left flank. AOK 15 was virtually destroyed and a huge gap was torn between Heeresgruppe B and Heeresgruppe G, through which poured two US corps. In a matter of days American pincers were closing around the Ruhr and Model lacked the reserves to stop them from linking up. Model preferred to evacuate the Ruhr and withdraw eastwards to continue resistance in the Harz Mountains, but Hitler forbade retreat and designated Germany's industrial heartland as 'Festung Ruhr'. Ever the professional soldier, Model obeyed and reoriented PzAOK 5 to protect the southern flank of the Ruhr along the river Sieg, but the Americans – enjoying complete air superiority and a massive advantage in mobility over the Germans – simply raced around the Ruhr. Despite heavy fighting near Paderborn, the First and Ninth US Armies met at Lippstadt on the afternoon of 1 April. Virtually all of Heeresgruppe B, including Model and 14 divisions, were trapped inside the 130km-by-95km Ruhr Pocket. The Ruhr Pocket contained about 370,000 German military personnel, but barely 75,000 were armed. Furthermore, fuel and ammunition reserves were negligible. Since Heeresgruppe B lacked

Captured American troops, probably from the 106th Infantry Division, which had two of its regiments surrounded in the Schnee Eifel during the opening days of Operation *Wacht am Rhein*. Over 6,600 GIs were bagged – the largest surrender of American troops in the ETO (European Theatre of Operations) and Model's last triumph. (Bundesarchiv, Bild 183-J28589, Fotograf. Büschel)

the strength to break out of this pocket, Kesselring airily told Model that the 11. Armee (AOK 11), rebuilding in central Germany, would mount a relief operation in two weeks, but Model knew that this was illusory. Once Heeresgruppe B was surrounded, the Americans were content to slowly squeeze the pocket from north and south while their armoured spearheads raced eastwards to meet the Soviets on the river Elbe.

Initially, Model's troops put up fierce resistance along the Dortmund–Ems Canal and the river Sieg from 4–9 April, and even managed one last counter-attack against the Ninth US Army near Dortmund. However, morale inside the pocket plummeted once it became obvious that Germany was being overrun. Model's staff tried to persuade him to open surrender talks with the Allies, but he would have none of it. By 11 April the Ninth US Army captured Essen and German resistance faded. Morale cracked in the Ruhr Pocket two days later, and Model suddenly lost contact with most of his subordinate formations and commanders. On 14 April, Zangen surrendered AOK 15. As his command disintegrated around him, Model decided to dissolve Heeresgruppe B on 15 April, instructing subordinate commanders to make their own decisions, whether to try and break out to the east or surrender. He instructed the Volksturm to simply discard their uniforms and go home. That same day, Major-General Matthew Ridgway, commander of the American XVIII Airborne Corps, sent Model a personal request under a flag of truce to surrender. Model replied that he was still bound by his oath to the Führer and refused to consider the offer. Eventually, 317,000 German troops from the Ruhr Pocket – including 24 generals – surrendered.

Once Heeresgruppe B was gone, Model spent the next four days on the run with a small column consisting of an Sd. Kfz. 234 heavy armoured car, an Opel Blitz radio truck and a DKW-sedan. He hoped to slip through American lines to reach the Harz Mountains, but this proved impossible. Other small groups of German troops were still armed in the Ruhr Pocket and Model encountered one, whose squad leader asked him what they should do. Model replied, 'Go home boys, the war is over for us,' then shook each one's hand and bid them luck. Model had already made the choice that he would commit suicide, as he suggested his old friend Friedrich Paulus should have done at Stalingrad rather than be handed over to the Soviets for a show trial. By the morning of 21 April 1945 Model was alone with Oberstleutnant Roger Michael, his Ic, in the woods near Wedau. He told Michael, 'You can bury me here,' then walked alone into the woods, drew his pistol and ended his remarkable 36-year military career with a single shot to the head.

A German wire-laying detachment moving through a shattered town in the Rhineland in spring 1945. Hitler refused to allow Heeresgruppe B to withdraw behind the Rhine, forcing Model to squander his remaining forces in a hopeless battle of attrition on the western side of the river. (Ian Barter)

OPPOSING COMMANDERS

Model spent the bulk of the war fighting the Soviets, with his principal opponents being Generals Georgy Zhukov, Ivan Konev and Konstantin Rokossovsky, who were among the best Red Army combat leaders. All three Soviet opponents were 5–6 years younger than Model and they did not have the depth of experience that he had gained prior to meeting them in combat. Zhukov was certainly Model's best all-round opponent, with significant experience in operational planning at Stavka, along with his famous battlefield victory over the Japanese at Khalkhin Gol in August 1939. However, Zhukov could be pig-headed about continuing attacks that had obviously failed, which cost the Red Army dearly when he fought Model in the 'Rzhev meatgrinder'. In contrast, Model made every effort to minimize losses among his troops during Operation *Zitadelle*, and once it was apparent that a breakthrough could not be achieved he did not keep throwing troops into hopeless attacks. Rokossovsky proved very tough on the defence at Moscow and Kursk, but he was also prone to commit his armour too quickly when on the offense – which enabled Model to react accordingly with his own limited reserves and therefore avoid encirclement. Indeed, although all three Soviet commanders were able to push Model's forces back during the campaigns of 1942–44, they never succeeded in surrounding and destroying any substantial German forces under his command.

During his last year of the war, Model's opponents on the Western Front included Britain's Field Marshall Bernard Montgomery and the American Lieutenant-Generals Omar Bradley and Courtney Hodges. Montgomery was clearly the most experienced and skilled of Model's Allied opponents, having gained considerable combat and staff experience in World War I, which had turned him into a thoroughly professional soldier. Montgomery made his mark in North Africa and then Italy as commander of Eighth Army, and by the summer of 1944 he had gained a good understanding of German defensive tactics. Armed with this experience, along with ULTRA decrypts, air superiority and a plentiful reserve of American-built tanks, Montgomery proved capable of mounting set-piece offensives that could grind down even the best German defences. However, success made Montgomery incautious when up against Model in the autumn of 1944, and he was slow to realize that the Wehrmacht's fighting spirit was not yet broken. When Montgomery ignored warnings about German armour in Holland, Model was quick to seize the opportunity to smash the British 1st Airborne Division – which led Montgomery to resort to a more cautious approach in the 1945 campaign.

In contrast to Montgomery and the Red Army generals, Model's American opponents were rank amateurs with negligible combat experience. As commander of 12th Army Group, Bradley had no combat experience at all prior to 1943 and then only a brief stint as a corps commander in Italy and Sicily. Despite inflated claims by correspondent Ernie Pyle that Bradley was 'the GI General', Bradley had nothing like Model's ability to relate to common soldiers and he was ignorant about the front-line realities facing

his troops in the autumn of 1944. Hodges, a West Point dropout, briefly distinguished himself as a junior infantry officer in the final months of combat in 1918, but made his name primarily as a trainer of infantrymen. Like Bradley, Hodges was thrust into high-level command without adequate experience at lower levels and failed to develop the kind of combat instincts that Model had learned in two wars. Despite their infantry credentials from Fort Benning, neither Bradley nor Hodges could appreciate the difficulty of fighting in the Hürtgen Forest and were content to send infantry divisions in piecemeal to be decimated. In the Ardennes, *Wacht am Rhein* caught both men flat footed and then they failed to react quickly in a crisis – totally the opposite of Model's behavior at Rzhev. It is probably fair to say that Bradley and Hodges were totally outclassed as military leaders by Walther Model.

German pioneers laying *Teller* anti-tank mines on a trail in the Hürtgen Forest, November 1944. The Allies' willingness to fight in poor terrain and weather conditions, which negated their advantages in mobility and air support, enabled Model to cobble together an effective defence in the Hürtgen Forest that inflicted great material and psychological damage on the ineptly led First US Army. (Ian Barter)

Model fought some of the best commanders that the enemy had to offer and he is the only one of Hitler's generals who could claim to have defeated Zhukov, Montgomery and Bradley. While Model was unable to inflict more than tactical reverses upon his opponents, they were often painful and humiliating setbacks that served to demonstrate that German forces operating under his command could be destroyed piece by piece, but they were never defeated.

INSIDE THE MIND

Model stood up to Hitler in a way that hardly anyone else dared and even refused to carry out orders with which he did not agree.
General der Panzertruppen Hasso von Manteuffel

Walther Model left no memoirs and he burned most of his personal papers in the Ruhr Pocket before committing suicide. However, based upon his actions and recorded statements, it is possible to deduce a great deal about Model's thoughts on military leadership. First and foremost, he was a very 'hands-on' commander who wanted to know his troops, his subordinates and the terrain on which they had to fight at first hand. During the defence of the Rzhev salient he knew virtually every battalion commander in AOK 9 and was familiar with the terrain in their sectors. He believed in *Anschauen* (personal inspection) not only to ensure that his orders were properly carried out, but to ensure that sufficient resources were allocated to guarantee mission success. With his experience as an adjutant in World War I, he also got involved in directing which units received replacements and where key officers would be assigned. This type of leadership style was perceived as micro-management by some German officers – such as Mellenthin – yet Model was willing to delegate when subordinates had earned his trust. Indeed, he was fortunate for most of his career from 1942–45 in having subordinates such as Harpe, Viettinghoff, Rendulic, Student and Bittrich, who were competent and reliable. Model also believed in front-line leadership – as did Rommel and Guderian – and visited critical sectors on a daily basis to assess the capabilities of his troops as well as enemy activity. Although Model's staff despaired of keeping track of his hyperactive wanderings – which sometimes left him out of communications for hours – he gained superb situational awareness and was not caught by surprise until Remagen Bridge was captured in 1945. Model also believed strongly in *Vorhalten* (prior planning). The successful defence of the Rzhev salient against Zhukov's Operation *Mars* was no fluke; Model spent weeks organizing his limited armour into *Kampfgruppen* near the expected Soviet attack sectors. He demonstrated his skill at *Vorhalten* once again during Operation *Büffel*.

Model's method of stopping Soviet offensives was based upon the close coordination of three factors, which would today be called battlefield operating systems. First was intelligence collection and analysis, which he directed to build up his situational awareness to identify likely enemy courses of action. Second was counter-mobility efforts designed to detect and impede any Soviet advance, based upon the construction of a continuous front and multiple rearward switch lines. Third was fire support, which was centralized to enable Model to concentrate it against the most dangerous threats. A fourth – manoeuvre – could also be included since Model preferred to use tactical reserves to counter-attack and recover lost terrain when this was feasible. Model's championing of a continuous front line was not well

German infantry moving into the Hürtgen Forest, September 1944. The murky, gloomy and wet environment of the forest acted as a force multiplier for Model and concealed the fact that his troops were badly outnumbered by the First US Army. (Ian Barter)

received by many officers in the Ostheer, since they preferred the strongpoint method adopted by most German units in the winter of 1941–42. A continuous line was rough on the troops in winter, forcing them to spend longer periods outdoors and exposing small units to destruction. However, a continuous front meant that Soviet units could not simply slip through gaps without being spotted and then targeted by German artillery. In return, troops dispersed on a continuous front in squad-size positions presented far less tempting a target for Soviet artillery than company- and battalion-size strongpoints. By visiting his troops on a daily basis, Model ensured that the continuous line was adopted and that units built adequate fieldworks, obstacles and minefields to give them a chance of surviving Soviet attacks. Model remained an infantryman through and through and he ensured that his infantry conducted aggressive patrols to take prisoners and gain information on enemy activities, which other German senior commanders often failed to enforce. He would never have tolerated the 'rest area' mentality that Hodges and Bradley allowed in the Ardennes because he could not afford to relax his vigilance.

Model enjoyed a very good relationship with Hitler and other Nazi leaders throughout his period as a senior commander and he never became involved with the resistance. He simply didn't care about politics unless it could get him more troops. Yet Model was far from sycophantic – he was one of the few senior commanders who would stand up to Hitler – and he was willing to ignore orders from the Führer when it suited him, such as building the Hagen Stellung in 1943 and deliberately restricting the use of 'scorched earth' tactics in the Ruhr to deny facilities to the victorious Allies.

In terms of personality, Model was sustained by a deep-rooted sense of German nationalism, his Lutheran faith and a belief in his own abilities. Except at the very end, in the Ruhr Pocket, when he knew the war was lost,

Generalfeldmarschall Model personally thanks Hitler Youth leaders who helped to dig field works and erect obstacles around Aachen in October 1944. Unlike most senior German officers, Model maintained the ability to relate to front-line troops throughout his career. (Bundesarchiv, Bild 183-J28036, Fotograf: Jäger)

Model was an energetic, indefatigable and aggressive leader. Confronted with crisis after crisis in 1942–45, he adopted a 'never say die' attitude and was never apathetic or at a loss during a crisis. He was also personally fearless and was wounded five times during the course of his military career. Model had developed a wry sense of humour as a junior officer in the trenches of World War I and he learned that humour was an effective tool for relieving tension and demonstrating to subordinates that he could be calm under pressure. Model also could be highly sarcastic, which he made little effort to conceal from others. During a conference at the OKH in January 1944, Hitler asked Model where he thought the Allies would land, in the Pas de Calais or Normandy. Model replied: 'In Portugal.' Many of the comments about Model's 'coarse' and 'uncouth' behavior are based on his infantryman's vernacular – which appeared rough to some of the more 'genteel' Generalstab officers – and his unsparing sense of humour. Unlike Manstein, however, he never mocked either the Führer or his commanders in front of subordinates. On the negative side, Model's optimism and 'can-do' attitude could go past the point of reason at times, which he bordered on during his tenure in Heeresgruppe Nord. Yet Model cared about his men, and while he would sacrifice rearguards when necessary, he never treated his troops like cannon fodder and made every effort to understand their conditions. In return, the common soldiers knew that Model was a competent commander who knew his business. He also had the ability to snatch victory from the jaws of defeat, which inspired his troops and created the saying: 'Where Model is present, nothing can go wrong.'

A LIFE IN WORDS

Walther Model did not survive the war to write his memoirs, thus his legacy was written by those of his peers and subordinates that did survive. Typically, Model is remembered as a fine tactician and stubborn defensive commander, but his detractors – of whom there were many – tend to define him as sycophantic if not servile to Hitler, lacking the operational brilliance of Manstein or the charisma of Rommel. A number of staff officers claimed that he had uncouth speech and manners and that he was brutal, cold and ruthless. Despite being accepted by some historians for decades, these subjective assessments about Walther Model's leadership are at best unsubstantiated and at worst the result of bias.

How was Model viewed by his superiors? Hitler openly referred to him as 'my best field marshal' and as the 'the saviour of the Eastern Front'. Model was loyal, aggressive and he produced results, which were endearing qualities to Hitler, and he rewarded Model with much greater latitude than other senior German commanders. Indeed, Model was the only German commander on the Eastern Front who was allowed to conduct a major withdrawal (Operation *Büffel*) while not under attack. Hitler also respected a hard-bitten front-line fighter like Model, who was so different from the 'Zossen staff types' that Hitler despised in the Generalstab (Zossen was the location south of Berlin where most of the OKH/OKW staff were located in two large underground bunkers). Josef Goebbels also commented favourably about Model in his diary, noting that he was the only general asking the Propagandaministerium (Propaganda Ministry) for more political materials to be sent to educate front-line troops. In fact, Model's troops in the Rzhev salient were probably lining their boots with Goebbels' articles, but Model realized that this kind of request earned him points with the Nazi leadership, which he could then translate into getting priority for replacements.

How was Model viewed by his peers and subordinates? Although Heinz Guderian worked well with Model, he is only briefly mentioned in *Panzer Leader* (1950), but Guderian does praise his 'correct deductions' at Kursk as well as his 'courageous' performance in Poland in 1944. Erich von Manstein barely mentioned Model in *Verlorene Siege* (*Lost Victories*) (1955), which is not surprising since Manstein was replaced by Model after his relief in March 1944. It was not until Friedrich Wilhelm von Mellenthin wrote *Panzerschlachten* (*Panzer Battles*) (1956) that non-German readers were given any real insight into Model's accomplishments or personality, but Mellenthin had more than a few axes to grind. Mellenthin was a sycophantic admirer of Manstein and resented Model replacing him, referring to him as 'an alert, dapper, fiery little man ... and although a soldier of great driving power and energy, yet he could hardly be regarded as an adequate substitute for Manstein.' Mellenthin, like other Generalstab officers, also resented Model's tendency to visit infantry units and get involved in tactical details, as well as dragging his staff along with him in the mud, rain and snow. In contrast, Manstein preferred to stay back in a nice chateau playing nightly bridge games with his staff. Mellenthin made no effort to point out that he never actually served on Model's staff. After Model was dead, many of those officers that opposed Hitler and survived to tell about it labelled him as a Nazi because of his unflagging loyalty to the regime. Yet Oberst Günther Reichhelm, who served on Model's staff as the Id (assistant operations officer) in AOK 9 at Rzhev and then the Ia (operations officer) of Heeresgruppe B for the last seven months of the war, had a far more enlightening assessment of Model. While candidly noting some of Model's flaws, he viewed him as a 'warm-hearted and intelligent leader' and rated him as 'one of the most outstanding soldiers of World War II'.

Finally, how have historians viewed Model? Liddell Hart complimented Model by saying that he had 'the amazing capability to collect a reserve from an almost empty battlefield'. After the defeat at Arnhem, it was easier for British historians to credit Model for skill in forming ad hoc combat units than acknowledging that Montgomery had made a gross error of judgment. While a few Western historians have given Model some credit for 'the September Miracle' in the West, most tend to fob him off merely as 'a zealous disciple of Hitler' as John Toland did. Even recently, the British historian Max Hastings wrote that, 'For all Model's competence as a commander, his behaviour ... reflected a refusal to confront reality.' These glib assessments really only cover Model's unwillingness to admit defeat in the last few months of the war and are silent about his accomplishments on the Eastern Front. Hastings ignores the fact that senior German commanders who 'confronted reality' in February 1945 either found themselves relieved or confronting a firing squad. Model was astute enough to avoid both fates. In contrast to these narrow Anglo-American interpretations of Model's contributions, the German historian Paul Carell noted Model's unique role, stating that 'never before in the war had Hitler entrusted so much military responsibility to one man'. This responsibility was not given lightly, but was earned at Rzhev, Orel, Tarnopol and Warsaw. Model's ability, demonstrated time and again, to overcome seemingly hopeless situations, along with his contribution to preventing a German collapse on both the Eastern and Western Fronts in the summer of 1944, is what sets him among the ranks of the great commanders of World War II.

FURTHER READING

Primary Sources at NARA

9. Armee, T312, Rolls 293–4, 296–7, 304, 320

XXXXI Armeekorps (mot.), T314, Rolls 981, 984–5

5. Panzer-Division, T315, Roll 271

3. Panzer-Division, T315, Roll 115

Chef des Technischen Amtes im Oberkommando des Heeres (OKH), T78

Secondary Sources

CMH Pub 104-1, *Military Improvisations during the Russian Campaign*, Washington, DC: Centre of Military History, 1983

Glantz, David M. and House, Jonathan M., *The Battle of Kursk*, Lawrence: University Press of Kansas, 1999

——, *Atlas of the Lublin-Brest Operation and the Advance on Warsaw*, 2005

Gorlitz, Walter, *Strategie der Defensive Model*, Munich: Limes Verlag, 1982

Leppa, Konrad, *Generalfeldmarschall Walter Model: Von Genthin bis vor Moskaus Tore*, Nurnberg: Prinz-Eugen Verlag, 1962

Newton, Steven H., *Hitler's Commander*, Cambridge, MA: Da Capo Press, 2005

Reichhelm, Oberst Gunther, *MS B701: Summary of Army Group B Engagements from the Middle of October 1944 until the Middle of April 1945*, US Army Foreign Military Studies, 29 November 1947

Rendulic, Lothar, *Gekämpft, Gesiegt, Geschlagen*, Heidelberg: Welsermühl Verlag, 1952

Stolfi, Russell H. S., 'The greatest encirclement in history: Link up of the German 3rd and 9th Panzer divisions on 15 September 1941 in the Central Ukraine' in RUSI Journal, December 1996

Wray, Timothy A., *Standing Fast: German Defensive Doctrine on the Russian Front During World War II*, Ft. Leavenworth, KS: Combat Studies Institute Research Survey No. 5, US Army Command & General Staff College, 1986

INDEX

References to illustrations are shown in **bold**.